JOHN CALVIN'S VIEW OF GOD'S LOVE AND THE DOCTRINE OF REPROBATION

by C. Matthew McMahon

COPYRIGHT INFORMATION

John Calvin's View of God's Love and the Doctrine of Reprobation by C. Matthew McMahon
Annexed is Calvin's work on the *Doctrine of Reprobation*
Edited by Therese B. McMahon

Some language and grammar has been updated in the annexed work from the original manuscript. Any change in wording or punctuation has not changed the intent or meaning of the original author(s), and has been made to aid the modern reader.

Published by Puritan Publications
A Ministry of A Puritan's Mind
3971 Browntown Road
Crossville, TN 38572
www.puritanshop.com
www.apuritansmind.com
www.puritanpublications.com

This Print Edition, 2015
Electronic Edition, 2015
Manufactured in the United States of America

ISBN: 978-1-62663-119-9
eISBN: 978-1-62663-118-2

TABLE OF CONTENTS

Table of Contents

CALVIN'S IMPACT ON THE REFORMATION AND WORLD

By C. Matthew McMahon, Ph.D., Th.D.

The impact of Calvin on the Reformation has been written about for centuries. It is no little task. Yes, one cannot appreciate any of Calvin's positions without understanding, at least in part, what kind of impact Calvin actually had in the world from his day to ours. He is not simply a figure in church history, or as commonly viewed, the "creator" of predestination. The sovereign God of the universe *used* John Calvin in such an enormous measure, one would think the entire fabric of our current social, political and economic society as we have come to know it today would have been radically changed. Calvin's impact is *enormous*.

Through a series of providences, God guided the little town of Geneva onto the scene of the Reformation to house one of the most influential theologians in the history of Christendom, or the world, *John Calvin*. There were a number of social, economic, political and religious matters that pressed the city to reform, and Calvin was involved in *each* area of this reform. Adult literacy was common, and Calvin's pen reached across the *socio-economic* barriers to affect all classes with sound teaching, especially through a renewed academic interest in the teachings of Augustine. Calvin was, in fact, theologically, an *Augustinian*. This trend of "learning" was already in motion before Calvin was ever born, and the ripe time of his commencement in ministry was providential as well. This new literacy began to overrun the priestly ignorance of those who obtained the position of priest, but were not formally trained well within the confines of the Roman Catholic Church. Though Calvin was not the most extroverted of people, the force of his theological and pastoral writing and preaching overthrew his demure countenance.

Calvin's educational life commenced in his tenure at the University of Paris. He attended the College de la Marche at the age of 14, then moved to the College de Montaigu, though some historical evidence is lacking to piece together exactly how these educational movements shifted, or if there is insufficient evidence to make the case that he ever attended Montaigu in the first place. It seems a summary of his stay in Paris may be said to, 1) have taught Latin grammar for a time, 2) then may have been formally affiliated with the College de Montaigu, and 3) studied arts (philosophy) there. It is sure that Calvin's father initially desired him to study *theology* in Paris, but then moved him to study law instead for future financial reasons. He was influenced greatly with Aristotelian philosophy here, something he would carry with him into his theological formulations seen in his commentary of Seneca's *de Clementia*, and in his *Institutes*, as well as being introduced into the school of Augustine's thought, which later carried over into the *Institutes*. There is overall, an uncertainty as to the exact nature of Calvin's sojourn in Paris, though through his writings and through the accounts of his life (especially Beza's *Life of John Calvin*) traces can be found to piece together a possible coherent "life of Calvin" during this period.

Calvin left Paris sometime in the 1520's with his degree in the arts in order to start his work at the university of Orleans in law (where he came face to face with an aspect of humanism that would shape his thinking for the rest of his life). The University of Orleans was not a collegiate university, and only had a course of study surrounding law (with a stress upon civil law) which had undergone radical revisions in 16th century France under the writings of men like Guillaume Bude. The humanism encountered here was not that of the 21st century, "man is the measure of all things without God," concept. Rather, it was, "how ideas were obtained and expressed," with an emphasis on going, "back to the sources," (*ad fontes*) concerning the meaning of a given word or idea. For instance, Erasmus, in his *Enchiridion*, said that the church ought to go back to the scriptures and the early fathers in order to reform itself (*i.e.* back to the *sources*). It was not, however, the intention for Calvin, at this time, to go back to commentaries, or the Latin text of the Bible, but the original sources, the Greek and Hebrew text of Scripture. Calvin's first formulations from these influences would demonstrate themselves after he had graduated Orleans in 1531, and then dedicated two years of his life to researching and writing his commentary of Seneca's *de Clementia*.

Calvin moved from humanist to reformer by a, "sudden conversion," (*subita conversione* as Calvin calls it). It was both revelatory for him (as with the manner in which he parallels his conversion with the Apostle Paul's in many ways) and enigmatic for any researcher of his life since little is given on that subject in his own writings. He left Paris after another stay for a time, went to Noyon, and then quit Noyon for Basel, thinking it wise to leave France for a time due to a tumultuous air surrounding the reformation that was underway through *other* reformers. Here, in his hermit-style retreat in Switzerland, he penned the first edition of the *Institutes* for French evangelicals. After this, he was forced to move back to France for a time in order to settle family affairs. He then decided to set out for Strasbourg, but the road there was hindered and he stopped over in the little city of Geneva to stay the night.

Reformation, at this time in history, was a *city-wide* phenomenon. First there was a sense of community in a given geographical area, second, economic and social struggles saw victory in partaking in the freedom of the Reformation, and thirdly, urban communities centered on the *doctrine of justification by faith alone.* There was a pressure to have a social change due to the circumstances of the times. It was not as though the "Hollywood" version of the stalwart reformer who stormed the city for the cause of reformation had historical veracity. Political, economic, social and military considerations were the cause of many of the Swiss Cantons to begin to embrace the "symbiotic" relationship of city and reformer. In the same manner, Geneva, for instance, would have such a relationship with Calvin as the Magistrate and Council would move ahead for the good of the political-religious state under the *guidance* of Calvin's theological-socio-economic writings and counsel. Calvin affected social and economic change, as well as theological reformation. And Geneva was primed and ready for this kind of relationship based on the history of a Swiss confederacy coming to light over the last sixty years before Calvin ever arrived, and then adopting many of the same reformation principles other Swiss cantons had already implemented. Farel, the city's former "reformer," cornered Calvin on his stay and convinced him to remain and continue the work. Unfortunately, his first tenure there did not go well and in 1538 he was exiled (along with Farel and Courault) due to a practical difference in implementing the Lord's Supper to wayward and unruly members of the city, though the city Council *insisted* they allow them to partake. Calvin refused. He spent three years in exile (1538-1541) where he wrote a new version of the *Institutes*, as well as a tract against the Catholics for intruding into Geneva during his absence in his *Reply to Sadoleto*. In 1541 he returned reluctantly, again by Farel's pressure, to continue what God had started through him.

Calvin, upon his return to Geneva after his Strasbourg exile, formulated a church-state relationship with the Magistrate of the city, or the senate, much like the Graeco-Roman city-state. The *Institutes* remain his theological powerhouse of reform, but his *Ecclesiastical Ordinances* (written in 1541 for the express purpose of structuring discipline and orderliness in Geneva) was the backbone of this ecclesiastical organization. This consistory was created in order to "police" religious orthodoxy. Such trials as the "Servetus affair" demonstrated the civil-religious power of the Consistory when they burned Servetus at the stake for heresy, and this has certainly "colored" Calvin's posthumous character for the last 450 years. However, as other countries and cantons had acted in the same manner with heretics, so the Genevan Council felt *obligated* to uphold the same religious convictions with burning Servetus at the stake. Yet, Calvin's role in all this was more akin to a technical advisor or expert witness rather than the prosecutor, which was left in the hands of Geneva's civil authorities. If Servetus had remained in the Catholic's hand, from whom he escaped, they would equally have burned him at the stake for his denial of critical Christian doctrine, such as the existence of the Trinity. Though this mark upon "the Reformation" stands in the sight of its critics, Calvin can be said to be exceedingly successful in his subsequent work during his time in Geneva (over the paralleled work of Vadian in the city of St. Gallen who had a different idea of reformation, though similar circumstances as Calvin).

The reformation was primarily the *work of God* through the *Word of God*. This idea was Calvin's maxim of success. Though he wrestled with the theological idea of accommodation (*i.e.* that God accommodates ideas to us as the Word of God in order to allow finite creatures to understand an infinite deity of incomprehensible dimensions) he concluded that God knows his audience, and in this way adjusts his language accordingly for such an audience to apprehend (not comprehend) truths about Him. This accommodation will be seen in the following chapter on the manner in which Calvin expresses his understanding of God's love. For Calvin, he used three aspects of God as father, teacher and judge to communicate to us His divine person. As a result, Calvin published many works attempting to help the people of God understand theology, especially in the French tongue (in which he published his *Institutes* in 1541 eclipsing the work of Luther, Melancthon and Zwingli as *the document* of the Protestant Reformation).

Concerning the message of Calvin's Christianity found in the *Institutes*, one does not find a basic central core doctrine from which all others emerge. Calvin's main doctrine is *not* predestination. Rather, Calvin's *Institutes* demonstrate a cogency *about* biblical doctrine *as a whole*, and the *Bible as a whole* affecting the Christian's view of *Jesus Christ* and every doctrine connected to Christ. Christ, then, should be said to be the center of Calvin's *thought*, but many *doctrines* surround Him as the central figure of God's redemptive history. Book 1 demonstrates the idea of how human beings can know anything about God. Book 2 demonstrates how human beings know God surrounding the person and redeemer Jesus Christ. Book 3 demonstrates how human beings obtain favor, blessing, grace, benefits and effects of grace through the redeemer Jesus Christ. Book 4 centers around the remaining theological issues of the church itself, and the outward means by which the church is called into fellowship with Jesus Christ.

Though Calvin did not return to France, he did affect the country for the Reformation in a variety of ways. Calvin, along with the city of Berne, attempted to press French diplomats to remove persecution of evangelicals. Geneva subsequently became a haven for over six thousand refugees from France to the single city of Geneva itself. Certainly Calvin's influence over the entire country remained primarily within the writings he published in French, affecting a number of socio-levels from 1540-45. Geneva even supplied pastors to needful French pastorates and by 1562

Calvinism was a dominant force throughout Protestant France.

Calvin became ill in 1564 with migraines, gout, pulmonary tuberculosis, intestinal parasites, thrombosed hemorrhoids, and irritated bowel syndrome. He died on Friday April 28, 1564. However, though Calvin was dead, his influence lived on – by 1575 Calvin's theology was established as an international religion. Though Luther affected the Reformation at its start, Calvin continued to hold the torch for years afterward primarily through his *Institutes*. Geneva itself became internationally known especially in light of its academic standing based on Calvin's work previously accomplished there. Here then we find *Calvinism* coming to light (a term first used by Joachim Westphal to refer primarily to the sacramental views of difference between the Reformed and the Lutherans). It culminated through the systematization of the Biblical record defending itself against Roman Catholicism – the premier theological force against Protestantism of the day. Calvin's influence became more recognized by the *Institutes* concerning his doctrine of salvation seen in both election and the doctrines of Grace, otherwise formulated by the synod in Dordtrecht in the acronym TULIP (Dordt convened from 1618 to 1619 against Remonstrant influences built upon Romish Doctrines and popularized by Jacobus Harmenszoon, *i.e.* Jacob Arminius).

Since Calvinism was a thoroughly biblical attempt to explain the Bible, it is impossible that we should neglect looking at its affect in a global sphere. Calvinism affects people not only theologically, but practically as well, so that Christ's glory is more clearly and people are transformed (reformed) in his image. Interesting enough Calvinism also affected the merchant trade in its capitalistic endeavors, though Calvin did not necessarily enforce capitalism. There was a struggle in Geneva around the effect of Calvinism on capitalism that parleyed between tradition and progress. Though various parties desired their own course of action based on class and status, there was a growing need to create "independent sources of capital" and a need to maintain "political independence" in the city. Calvinism, then, harnessed industry, though Calvin did not develop a kind of *economic theory*. Later, during the 17th century, Calvinism and capitalism "were virtually coextensive." Weber maintains that this was due to the Calvinistic doctrine of "calling" (not "effectual calling," but of vocation (*i.e.* what would a Christian do in God's calling for his life)). This idea was placed in a more concrete position through federal theology which emphasized not only the salvation of the individual through grace in Christ, but also what that individual would do in laboring before God and unto God in the world.

Calvinism has had a profound effect on the nations of the West, especially on *culture*. Three aspects stand out: 1) the international character of the movement affecting religious, economic and political issues in those countries; 2) the "world affirming character" of Calvin's theology especially as developed later by the Puritans; 3) even in the midst of its dematerialization amidst secular culture, its residue remained to influence secular society. Even American religious communities, as they came over from both Dutch and English countries, settled in America to create godly commonwealths under a covenant with God. In this way, since Calvinism touches upon *every* sphere of society, (and not simply the doctrines of grace), to study the movement is not to lean upon its historical past, but to study current political, social, and religious events and further observe its impact on culture throughout the world.

CALVIN, GOD'S LOVE AND THE DOCTRINE OF REPROBATION

by C. Matthew McMahon, Ph.D., Th.D.

Calvin undertook the formal topic surrounding accommodation (known by later reformers such as Francis Turretin as "the compound and divided senses of the Scriptures" which is far more helpful) through the employed term "after the manner of men" in dealing with difficult texts that demonstrate tension to the reader of Scripture. God speaks to men in the bible "after the manner of men" – which, in my own opinion, is a very cryptic phrase for Calvin to use. In academia such phrases as "God Accommodating Himself to Human Capacity"[1] are used to describe Calvin's position on this tension. In this light of accommodation, how does Calvin reconcile the apparent conflict between God's eternal predestination of men to heaven or hell, and the Fatherly love that Calvin triumphs over throughout His writings which equally follows all men? How can God eternally damn

---

[1] Battles, Ford Lewis, *Interpreting John Calvin*, (Grand Rapids: Baker Books, 1996), 124ff.

some men, yet love them at the same time? Did Calvin believe God had two different wills operating at the same time?[2]

Concerning God's love Calvin says, *"Proofs of the love of God towards the whole human race exist innumerable,* all which demonstrate the ingratitude of those who perish or come "to perdition." This fact, however, forms no reason whatever why God should not confine His especial or peculiar love to a few, whom He has, in infinite condescension, been pleased to choose out of the rest!"[3] Calvin said concerning John 3:16, "...the whole matter of our salvation must not be sought any where else than in Christ, so we must see whence Christ came to us, and why he was offered to be our Savior. Both points are distinctly stated to us. Namely, that faith in Christ brings life to all, and that Christ brought life, *because the Heavenly Father loves the human race, and wishes that they should not perish.*"[4] Calvin also says,

---

[2] For a full discussion of this, see my work, "The Two Wills of God."

[3] Calvin, John, *Calvin's Calvinism*, <u>A Treatise on the Eternal Predestination of God and the Secret Providence of God</u>, translated by Henry Cole, (Grandville: Reformed Free Publishing Association, 1950), 268. (Emphasis Mine.)

[4] Calvin, John, *Calvin's Commentaries Volume 17*, <u>Harmony of Matthew, Mark, Luke; and John 1-11</u>, (Grand Rapids: Baker Book House, 1996), 122-123. (Emphasis Mine.)

"[God] has employed the universal term *whosoever, both to invite all indiscriminately to partake of life, and to cut off every excuse from unbelievers...yet he shows himself to be reconciled to the whole world, when he invites all men without exception to the faith of Christ, which is nothing else than an entrance into life.*"[5] Calvin also demonstrates the tension when he states concerning Ezekiel 18:23, "We hold, then, that; God wills not the death of a sinner, since he calls all equally to repentance, and promises himself prepared to receive them if they only seriously repent...that God always wishes the same thing, though by different ways, and in a manner inscrutable to us. Although, therefore, God's will is simple, yet great variety is involved in it, as far as our senses are concerned. Besides, it is not surprising that our eyes should be blinded by intense light, so that we cannot certainly judge how God wishes all to be saved, and yet has devoted all the reprobate to eternal destruction, and wishes them to perish."[6]

Though Calvin never believed that God's will was "complex" he did believe that there are certain

---

[5] Ibid, 124- 125.

[6] Calvin, John, *Calvin's Commentaries Volume 12*, Ezekiel 13-20 and Daniel 1-6, (Grand Rapids: Baker Book House, 1996), 246-248. (Emphasis Mine.)

senses which must be applied to a passage in order to understand it. That is where he says God wills certain things but in different "ways." Calvin believed His will was simple, one instantaneous act, unified and complete. He also says it is "inscrutable to us" which shows the utter infinite and boundless dimension which the mind of God understands all things simply. He will use words like, "immutable goodwill of God,"[7] "all-efficacious is the will of God"[8] and that a "twofold will of God...is by no means admitted by us."[9] Calvin makes the necessary distinction between the senses or "ways" in which the Bible explains concepts to men as creatures.

In the work against Pighius, *The Bondage and Liberation of the Will: A Defense of the Orthodox Doctrine of Human Choice against Pighius*, Calvin is fighting against Pelagianism. Pighius had taken up the Pelagian's position which gave birth to some of the opinions such as God willing *all men to be saved* in either of the Biblical

---

[7] Calvin, John, *Calvin's Calvinism*, A Treatise on the Eternal Predestination of God and the Secret Providence of God, translated by Henry Cole, (Grandville: Reformed Free Publishing Association, 1950), 28.
[8] Ibid, 43.
[9] Ibid, 114.

senses. They are in unison on the topics of the desire of God for the salvation of all men, and on the Gospel call being extended sincerely to all men in the compound sense – which is a mistake. It is the problem of reconciling the two wills which stems from this Hegelian-like schematic. Calvin condemns Pighius and the erroneous doctrine of free-will, labeling it as the, "undiluted expression of Pelagian ungodliness."[10] Calvin believed Pighius' doctrine was in direct opposition to the Council of Orange's anathema to mark Pelagianism as heresy. He says, "If anyone teaches that both the increase and beginning of faith and the very desire to believe [come] not as a gift of grace (*i.e.*, through the working of the Holy Spirit reforming our will from unbelief to belief, from irreligion to religion), but are innate in us by nature," he is declared to be a heretic by a decree of a church council...he is condemned as an adversary of the Holy Spirit."[11] Calvin even goes so far to say that Pighius is the "ghost writer" for Pelagius. Calvin believed that Pelagianism and

---

[10] Calvin, John, *The Bondage and Liberation of the Will: A Defence of the Orthodox Doctrine of Human Choice against Pighius*, Edited by A.N.S. Lane, Translated by G.I. Davies, (Grand Rapids: Baker Books, 1996), 104.
[11] Ibid, 188.

Semi-Pelagianism made God a debtor to man.[12] Calvin was not going to give one *iota* to the prevailing heresy which Pighius was propagating because he knew where it would lead. It is the immediate contradiction to election and reprobation.

Calvin makes the point that God only reveals salvation to some men, and then hardens others by His express will and good pleasure in the compound sense (his will of decree). He says, "He promises through Isaiah that he will be found by those who have not sought him, and that he will appear and show himself to those who were not concerned to know him. Did he bestow this benefit on all? By common consent he bestowed it only on some."[13] Calvin asks this of Pighius as a rhetorical question which is answered with a categorical, "no." Men must be drawn of Christ and they must be laden with recognizable sin. They cannot come proud or righteous, they must be made to see their wickedness. Calvin says, "Therefore for Christ to reveal himself to you as your doctor you must recognize your disease."[14] Calvin says that Pighius has run into

---

[12] Ibid, 189ff.
[13] Ibid, 192.
[14] Ibid, 193.

absurdity to believe that God's grace in salvation is equally offered to all. What Calvin means is that effectual calling, or the gift of grace is not *given* to all. Speaking of Pighius, "What then is the reason why he rushes headlong, as if with eyes shut, into such great absurdity? It is of course just this, that once he has conceived the idea in his mind that the grace of God is offered equally to all, provided that they show themselves to be worthy of it, he is held prisoner of this idea, so that he is incapable of further perception or judgment."[15] But this he was attempting to prove in the compound sense. Pighius had contracted the Pelagian virus which not only stated that men were able to save themselves, but that God offered salvation to all because He desired their salvation.

Pighius rejected Calvin's view and questioned the sincerity of the free offer to the reprobate in almost the same way that those who create a double will in God do. He could not understand how Calvin could reconcile the indiscriminate preaching with the problem. Calvin answers with the classic biblical and reformed answer that *God makes men inexcusable.* "But [asks Pighius] what about the reprobate, to whom

---

[15] Ibid, 198.

nothing is offered except the dead letter? My reply is that it is indeed characteristic of God's instruction that it should bring salvation to those who hear it, but when it has fulfilled this function in believers a punishment is ready for those who are rebellious and obstinate. Yet Pighius supposes that God wants all to be corrected and therefore offers his help equally to all - so it is within our power to assent or refuse."[16] In his sermons on reprobation and election[17], Calvin is emphatic that God makes men inexcusable with the preaching of the Word of God. Preaching is two-fold to Calvin, "be it to draw his elect unto him, or to make other[s] inexcusable."[18] Pighius would then begin to use varied Scriptures such as Ezekiel 18:23, 32 and 33:11 to "prove" that God has this unfeigned desire towards the reprobate for their salvation. But Calvin says that when men run to these Scriptures, they should think twice. He calls them "troublecoasts" who "maketh his

---

[16] Ibid, 214.

[17] In the work itself Calvin adds a short treatise called, "An Answer to certain slanders and blasphemies, wherewith certain evil disposed persons have gone about to bring the doctrine of God's everlasting predestination into hatred," which is based on Romans 9:20.

[18] John Calvin, *Sermons on Election and Reprobation*, (Audobon: Old Paths Publications, Originally Published in 1579, reprinted 1996), 306.

buckler" from these texts.[19] They attempt to make the Scriptures speak against God's *one* will and consequently promote *two* wills. Calvin shows this to be a grievous mistake. He goes so far to say it is a mistake that he equates God's will and the devil's will for the reprobate *as one*. He says, "God willeth the same thing that the devil doth,"[20] concerning the reprobate. All of this talk centered around the compound sense, not the divided sense, (God's preceptive will seen in Scripture as *law and command*).

---

[19] Ibid, 307.
[20] Ibid, 308.

CALVIN'S VIEW OF GOD'S DECREE

Calvin expands his ideas and theological views in the second treatise he compiles against Pighius, and others such as Georgias, who hold to Pelagian views of election and reprobation; specifically those views which extend into what the "double will" men believe. The work is entitled *A Treatise on the Eternal Predestination of God.*

In the compound sense (demonstrating God's eternal decree), Calvin does *not* believe that *anyone* can come to Christ and be saved. In this way, he did not believe the promises of God are for *all men*, though they are tendered to all men in preaching which is the outward will of the divided sense (how God accommodates Himself in the Word to finite men who hear the good news of the Gospel). "This fellow also maintains that all men, generally and equally, are "drawn" of God; and that there is no difference, except where resistance begins it; and that when God promises that he will make "hearts of flesh" out of "hearts of stone" nothing else is meant than the making us capable of receiving the grace of God; and that this

28

capability, or the being made capable, extends without distinction to the whole human race, whereas the *Scripture most clearly affirms that this is the peculiar privilege of the church of God.*"[21] Calvin does not believe it *can* be given to all. Though some theologians would like to *extend* it to all, Calvin says, "we say that it is by grace, or Divine predestination."[22] This may seem unfair to some, and Calvin rhetorically deals with the issue of "fairness" as he moves through Romans 9 more than once. But he says of the reprobate, "Again... Who created the reprobate but God? And why? Because He willed it. Why did He will it?—"Who art thou, O man, that replies against God?""[23]

Calvin also takes to task the improper notion of the "two wills of God." He cannot allow the character of God to be ruined by the idea that God can will something at one time and then not at another in a single sense; that would be contradictory. God cannot will something half-heartedly and not bring it to pass. In other words, Calvin wanted men to explain

---

[21] Calvin, John, *Calvin's Calvinism*, <u>A Treatise on the Eternal Predestination of God and the Secret Providence of God</u>, translated by Henry Cole, (Grandville: Reformed Free Publishing Association, 1950), 22. (Emphasis Mine.)
[22] Ibid, 39.
[23] Ibid, 40.

themselves in the senses they were speaking, and demonstrate a thorough knowledge of how accommodation worked in our finite understanding. The only place, here, that Calvin can be cited as violating such a principle, is that he explained it in cryptic terms that this writer does not find as helpful as it could have been communicated.

Pighius was wrong in both his accommodating senses. Calvin says, "This, however, is not true, if He willed some things and then did not. Nothing, therefore, is done but that which the Omnipotent willed to be done, either by permitting it to be done or by doing it Himself."[24] God cannot will one thing and do another, that would be a contradiction in Him and result in an eternal frustration. He cannot will the salvation of people He will never save. "The Scripture is replete with examples of the same nature and tendency. Shall we, then, on that account either impute the cause or fault of sin to God, or represent Him as having a double or twofold will, and thus make Him inconsistent with Himself?"[25] Pighius says that He *can* do this and does *in fact* do this. Calvin says otherwise,

---

[24] Ibid, 43.
[25] Ibid, 255.

"The fiction of Pighius is puerile and absurd, when he interprets grace to be God's goodness in inviting all men to salvation, though all were lost in Adam. For Paul most clearly separates the foreknown from those on whom God deigned not to look in mercy."[26] And also, "blindness is justly inflicted of God upon all reprobates generally."[27] There are those who use the grace and goodness of God as a blanket for all, and those, like Calvin, who say that God is only merciful, and reserves mercy, for some. But why does He do this? Why not save all men? Calvin says:

> If it be asked, Why He does not thus teach all men, in order that they may come to Christ? the answer is, because, those whom He does teach, He teaches in mercy; but those whom He does not teach, in judgment He teaches them not. For "He hath mercy on whom He will have mercy, and whom He will He hardeneth, (Rom. ix. 18). The sum of this sacred matter, however, may be compressed into a smaller compass still.

---

[26] Ibid, 47.
[27] Ibid, 162.

Christ does not say that those are drawn by the Father who have a flexible heart given them to render them able to come to Him; but that those who do come to Him are they whom God by His Spirit touches within, and who, under the efficacy of that touch, actually come. Now that this privilege is not given to all promiscuously is a fact which universal experience makes manifest, even to the blind.[28]

Calvin maintains correctly, "He predestines some to destruction from their very creation."[29] Not only does he predestine them from their very creation, but he makes their lives a filling up of sin to judge them on the Day of Wrath. "Most certainly nothing is here heard of Pighius' absurd prating – that grace is the same towards all, but that the goodness of God is the more brightly illustrated by His enduring the vessels of wrath while He suffers them to come to their own end...Now if this being "afore prepared unto glory "is peculiar and special to the elect, it evidently follows

---

[28] Ibid, 52-53.
[29] Ibid, 58.

that the rest, the non-elect, were equally "fitted to destruction," because, being left to their own nature, they were thereby devoted already to certain destruction. That they were "fitted to destruction, "by their own wickedness is an idea so silly that it needs no notice. It is indeed true that the reprobate procure to themselves the wrath of God, and that they daily hasten on the falling of its weight upon their own heads."[30] He also says, "There can be no real desire of doing good in men which does not proceed from God's election of them. The reprobate, however, made, as they are vessels unto dishonour, never cease to provoke the vengeance of God upon themselves; thereby manifestly proving, as in written characters, that they are ordained to destruction. To Pighius, however, such a doctrine is the very climax of absurdity."[31]

Where does unbelief come from? How do men die in their sins? Calvin answers Pighius by saying, "The secret and eternal purpose and counsel of God must be viewed as the original cause of their blindness and unbelief."[32] Calvin was quite orthodox when it came to the eternal counsel of God. He says, "The

---

[30] Ibid, 76-77.
[31] Ibid, 142.
[32] Ibid, 81.

unbelief of the world, therefore, ought not to astonish us, if even the wisest and most acute of men fail to believe. Hence, unless we would elude the plain and confessed meaning of the Evangelist, that few receive the Gospel, we must fully conclude that the cause is the will of God; and that the outward sound of that Gospel strikes the ear in vain until God is pleased to touch by it the heart within."[33] He also states, "I obtain thereby the next conclusion, that the mercy of God is offered equally to those who believe and to those who believe not, so that those who are not divinely taught within are only rendered inexcusable, not saved."[34] Calvin cannot believe that any man would confess God to offer the Gospel to all men in a desire to see them all saved in the compound sense. He says, "Now, a man must be utterly beside himself to assert that this promise is made to all men generally and indiscriminately."[35] Calvin knows the effectual Gospel call is only for the elect, not all men. "For if God willed, or wished, that His truth should be known unto all men, how was it that He did not proclaim and make known His law to

---

[33] Ibid, 82.
[34] Ibid, 93. It is important to note that the word "offered" here is the Latin use of the word. See footnote 86.
[35] Ibid, 100.

the Gentiles also?"[36] Calvin cannot fathom why God would desire all men to be saved, will that end, never bring it to pass because He has reprobated them from all eternity, and never give them the Gospel light as with many of the nations previous to Christ coming. This makes no sense to him, and it should not because it would violate the Bible rationally and logically. Calvin rebukes Pighius for thinking as such:

> What? Are we to suppose that the apostle did not know that he himself was prohibited by the Holy Spirit from "preaching the word "in Asia, and from passing over into Bithynia? But as the continuance of this argument would render us too prolix, we will be content with taking one position more. That God, "after having thus lighted the candle of eternal life to the Jews alone, suffered the Gentiles to wander for many ages in the darkness of ignorance; and that, at length, this special gift and blessing were promised to the Church:

---

[36] Ibid, 103.

"But the Lord shall arise upon thee; and His glory shall be seen upon thee"(Isa. lx. 2). Now let Pighius boast, if he can, that God willeth all men to be saved! The above arguments, founded on the Scriptures, prove that even the external preaching of the doctrine of salvation, which is very far inferior to the illumination of the Spirit, was not made of God common to all men... no one but a man deprived of his common sense and common judgment can believe that salvation was ordained by the secret counsel of God equally and indiscriminately for all men.[37]

The reason Pighius believes God should offer salvation to all men "equally" is because there is something intrinsic in man which God enjoys and delights in or loves. Pelagius taught that there was such an extent of goodness in men that God desired their salvation, though they committed wicked acts. They were not inherently evil, but only evil as they continued

---

[37] Ibid, 104-105.

to sin. Calvin did not believe such an idea. There is nothing in a depraved man which God loves or delights in. To Calvin, even in a saved man God delights in nothing except His own image and reflection which has been renewed in Christ no matter how faint or bright that may be. He says, "For the Scripture declares aloud, that whatever there is in fallen and corrupt man by nature is hateful in the sight of God. And it pronounces, with a voice equally loud, that nothing is acceptable to God but His own image in those who are created anew in Christ."[38] God is not pleased with men, He is pleased with Himself, and His elect servant Jesus Christ. Men are not acceptable to God in any other fashion other than fashioned *in Christ and His blood.* No work, no striving, no running, nothing is acceptable to God other than His own reflection and image. It was a denial of this that allowed men like Pelagius and Pighius to concoct their erroneous doctrines.

Calvin argued that God cannot be disappointed, ever, in the compound sense. If He were to will the salvation of the reprobate, and then not bestow the condition by whcih the reprobate may come to saving faith (which is justifying faith), then God would be

---

[38] Ibid, 118.

frustrated. "But Paul teaches us (continues Georgius) that God " would have all men to be saved." "It follows, therefore, according to his understanding of that passage, either that God is disappointed in His wishes, or that all men without exception must be saved."[39] This is Calvin using biblical logic. God cannot wish all men saved and not save them. That would be illogical, or "a contradiction." Calvin blatantly uses logic through his entire treatise. He not only uses logic, but also refrains from going outside the hermeneutic of consistency. He says, "If this worthless fellow goes on with his interpretation of the Scriptures at this rate, according to the letter, he will bye-and-bye fabricate for us a corporeal God, assigning as his reason, because the Scripture speaks of God as having ears, eyes, feet and hands. The meaning of the passage, however, is most simple and plain. That those are "blotted out of the book of life" who, having been considered for a time the children of God, as being among them, afterwards draw back and fall away into their own place, as Peter most truly describes Judas to have done."[40] When those who do not use logic in the study and application of the Scriptures, and argue against it, Calvin says they are,

---

[39] Ibid, 166.
[40] Ibid, 170.

"professedly laughing at all sound logic."[41] Calvin was as much a profound logician as the Apostle Paul, since he knew that men cannot know propositional truth without thinking *correctly*.

[41] Ibid, 326.

CALVIN'S VIEW OF GOD'S PROVIDENCE

Calvin also had much to say on God's providential dealings with the reprobate. The entire second half of the treatise is given to the topic. He begins by defining what providence is, "By Providence, we mean, not an unconcerned sitting of God in heaven, from which He merely observes the things that are done in the world; but that all-active and all-concerned seatedness on His throne above, by which He governs the world which He Himself hath made."[42] He believed that God was so powerful and so in control of all things that there are statements which he makes that could cause some "reformed" men to shudder. He says, "Those things which are vainly or unrighteously done by man are, rightly and righteously, the works of God!"[43] And this, "The sum and substance, however, of the whole Divine matter is this: Although men, like brute beasts confined by no chains, rush at random here and there, yet God by His secret bridle so holds and governs them, that they cannot move even one of their fingers without

---

[42] Ibid, 224.
[43] Ibid, 233.

accomplishing the work of God much more than their own!"[44] And this, "Moreover, God Himself very frequently makes use of the wicked to punish the sins of men, especially of His own people. And sometimes He drags them by the neck, as it were, to make them the instruments of His goodness to men and saints."[45] And he says, "What we maintain is, that when men act perversely, they do so (according to the testimony of the Scripture) by the ordaining purpose of God."[46] Calvin also believed the works of Satan were the works of God in a certain sense, "But what worketh Satan? In a certain sense, the work of God! That is, God, by holding Satan fast bound in obedience to His Providence, turns him whithersoever He will, and thus applies the great enemy's devices and attempts to the accomplishment of His own eternal purposes!"[47] He believes this to be true because of his maxim, "that God, in wondrous ways and in ways unknown to us, directs all things to the end that He wills, that His eternal WILL might be the FIRST CAUSE of all things."[48]

---

[44] Ibid, 238.
[45] Ibid, 239.
[46] Ibid, 242.
[47] Ibid, 240.
[48] Ibid, 190. (Emphasis his.)

Calvin believed that God causes men to do what they do.[49] That God is not only sovereign of the outer man, but also of the heart. When men sin God is not responsible for their sin, but He has certainly manipulated the emotion, desires, and circumstances to fulfill His good purpose by them. As with the hardening of Pharaoh's heart, Calvin believed it was the work of God. "And Moses positively affirms that the hardening of Pharaoh's heart was the work of God."[50] It cannot be any other but God in the working of the reprobate in such a detailed and providential manner. God must execute His will and decrees in all things He has ordained and appointed so that a certain end will take shape and come to pass. This end is ordained, and cannot be anything but ordained, and such ordination necessarily includes the works and will of the reprobate.

The greatest polemic work Calvin ever wrote, a cornerstone document of the Reformation, was the *Institutio Chrsitianae Religionis,* or *Institutes of the Christian Religion.* The full original title given to its revision in 1559 was *Institutes of the Christian Religion, now first*

---

[49] Ibid.
[50] Ibid, 241.

arranged in four books and divided by definite headings in a very convenient way. Also enlarged by so much added matter that it can be almost regarded as a new work. Calvin had set down in writing his mind on the Christian religion, and his understanding of the Scriptures in a "very convenient way" so that it would be readily accessible and easy to use by the Christian for edification. It is here that he directs the readers of his various works, whether treatises, commentaries or sermons, to come to his *Institutes* and gather his full mind on any subject, especially if the other works are written in "brevity" or may be confusing. Calvin rested on his *Institutes* and directed his readers to do the same. One should look to Calvin's *Institutes* in order to gain his full mind on the subject of election and reprobation. His treatises formerly quoted above are very helpful, but are more difficult to use due to their apologetic nature, and in some areas more incomplete as compared to the *Institutes.*[51]

---

[51] If Calvin himself did not urge his readers 4 or 5 times in his <u>Treatise on the Eternal Predestination of God and the Secret Providence of God</u> one would conclude that as a benchmark work on the subject. As a whole, that work is a longer treatment than the *Institutes* give on that topic. Yet, the *Institutes* are more systematically arranged, logically conceived, and easier to use on

Calvin, as with this writer, did *not* believe God had two wills. He knew that to ascribe to God two wills would be to contradict the nature of God and cause him to become a frustrated God; this would, in fact, be no God at all. Those passages that seem to show He has repented or changed his mind are vindicated by the reformer. Calvin says, "The sacred history does not show that God's decrees were abrogated when it relates that the destruction which had once been pronounced upon the Ninevites was remitted (Jonah 3:10); and that Hezekiah's life, after his death had been intimated, had been prolonged (Isaiah 38:5). Those who think so are deceived in these estimations."[52] Calvin may not be rightly using his accommodating terms here properly. It is impossible to ascribe a change in God's nature which is what happens when men ascribe a change in God's mind. God's will is simple and unified. Calvin shows this to be true when he deals with God "repenting." For God to truly have an emotional reaction to a given situation

---

the subject, which was why Calvin wanted his readers to search there before going to any of his other works.

[52] Calvin, John, *Institutes of the Christian Religion*, Volume 1, Edited by John T. McNeil, (Philadelphia: Westminster Press, 1960), 227. (1.17.14)

would destroy His immutability, and then the dominos fall from there. It would not matter if the act was in anger, repentance, pity, grief or jealousy. Calvin says, "First, God's repenting is several times mentioned, as when he repented of having created man (Gen. 6:6); of having put Saul over the kingdom (1 Sam. 15:1); and of his going to repent of the evil that he had determined to inflict upon his people, as soon as he sensed any change of heart in them (Jer. 18:8)...hence, many contend that God has not determined the affairs of men by an eternal decree, but that, according to each man's deserts or according as he deems him fair and just, he decrees this or that each year, each day, and each other...concerning repentance, we ought so to hold that it is no more chargeable against God than is ignorance, or error, or powerlessness. For if no one wittingly and willingly puts himself under the necessity of repentance, we shall not attribute repentance to God without saying either that he is ignorant of what is going to happen, or cannot escape it, or hastily and rashly rushes into a decision of which he immediately has to repent."[53] Calvin says we must take these things *figuratively*. If we take these things figuratively how do we ascribe them

---

[53] Ibid, 226. (1.17.12)

to God in this sense? Is language really adequate to describe God if this is the case? Would one fall into some type of Kantian *phenoumenal* world which is really unknown to them? Calvin explains, "Surely its meaning [repentance] is like that of all other modes of speaking, that describe God for us in human terms. For because our weakness to not attain to his exalted state, the description of him that is given to us must be accommodated to our capacity so that we may understand it. Not that the mode of accommodation is for him to represent himself to us not as he is in himself, but as he seems to us."[54] Here Calvin comments to the best of his ability in distinguishing the senses. The anthropomorphic nature of Scripture must never leave one's mind as they study God's word. God *never* repents, *never* gets angry, *never* is jealous, etc. He is without passions and emotions in the *compound* sense. If this fundamental point is missed, and one does not understand that God's Word to men is a mere lisping, or baby talk to weak creatures, one will continually ascribe to God far more than is warranted and fabricate something other than what He is by detracting from his perfection and nature. Calvin called

---

[54] Ibid, 227. (1.17.13)

this, "speaking after the manner of men." If one misses this point, one will pull Him down to humanity while they believe to be exalting His word.

Calvin teaches that God does not do anything which He does not first decree. And all His decrees will come to pass. God is so providentially involved in every aspect of creation, and all the affairs of men, "that men can accomplish nothing except by God's secret command, that they cannot by deliberating accomplish anything except what he has already decreed with himself and determines by his secret direction."[55] This immediate intervention in the lives of men moves into the realm of reprobation as it relates to their hardening. God is not a *deistic* god. He is involved with men so much that His decree concerning the color of their shirt today and the number of holes in it was determined before the foundation of the world. Their disposition, their emotional reactions, their heartfelt longings are all controlled and executed by His sovereign counsel. Voltaire disliked the idea of a cosmic voyeur peeping in through the keyhole of his life at every possible action. How much more would he have hated the fact that God not only looked within, but manipulated and

---

[55] Ibid, 229. (1.18.1)

sovereignly controlled his very heart! Calvin says, "Whatever we conceive of in our own minds is directed to his own end by God's secret inspiration."[56] This does not mean that God is acting in the actions of the wicked. Rather, it does mean that God so orders the circumstances that the wicked comply with their own desires to accomplish God's intended end. Such is the case with the two most heinous crimes every committed – the fall from the garden of Eden, and the crucifixion of Jesus Christ.

---

[56] Ibid, 231. (1.18.2) Calvin uses the following references for support: Ezek. 7:26; Job 12:24; Psalm 107:40; 106:40; Lev. 26:36; 1 Sam. 26:12; Isaiah 29:14; 29:10; Rom. 1:28; 1:20-24; Exodus 8:15; 9:12; 10:20; 11:10; 14:8; Psalm 105:25; Josh. 11:20; Deut. 2:30.

CALVIN'S VIEW OF HARDENING

Calvin agrees that God's will is the cause of men being hardened and reprobated. Concerning the hardening of Pharaoh he says, "God's will is posited as the cause of hardening."[57] God will even send, according to his purpose, delusions to the wicked that they *would* believe lies. How then could some really believe God wills the salvation of all when it expressly says that God deludes them in this sense? Calvin says that sometimes, "the working of error flows from God himself."[58] Calvin does admit that it is difficult to follow God's will sometimes, though he knows it never changes. He uses the illustration of a son who wishes his father would live, though he is sick, but God wills that he die.[59] The son was rightfully willing the life of his father, but that only meant he was being faithful to prayer as the duty of man prescribes. God's will still is secret in such matters to men.

Given the immutable and unchanging nature of God's will, Calvin shows that God does not will all men

---

[57] Ibid, 231. (1.18.2)
[58] Ibid, 232. (1.18.3)
[59] Ibid, 234. (1.18.3)

to be saved, since they are not. Calvin says, "If he will all to be saved, he would set his Son over them, and would engraft all into his body with the sacred bond of faith."[60] But God *does not* do this. He engrafts and saves only those for whom Christ died and no others. Calvin knows that God does not will the salvation of all because the biblical record ties the condition of faith upon the call. And dead men cannot believe unless they are regenerated. And men cannot be regenerated unless God sends His Spirit to them. And the Spirit is not sent if God had not called them. And if God had not called them then He has not predestined them to saving faith. And if this is so, then He has not willed them to be saved. It could not possibly be something they are able to do, but only what God is able to do. Calvin says, "If we turn our eyes to works, we wrong the apostle [in Romans 9:13] as if he did not see what is quite clear to us!"[61] Calvin did not believe that God had the same attitude towards all men and in this way could say with the apostle that He loves some and hates others. In the same section, Calvin asks this question concerning Romans 9:13, "Do you see how Paul

---

[60] Ibid, Volume 2, 946 (3.22.10)
[61] Ibid, Volume 2, 946. (3.22.11)

attributes both to God's decision alone?" He is rhetorical here and says, "If, then, we cannot determine a reason why he vouchsafes mercy to his own, except that it so pleases him, neither shall we have any reason for rejecting others, other than his will. For when it is said that God hardens or shows mercy to whom he wills, men are warned by this to seek no cause outside his will."[62]

Though this is the case with God's will, Calvin teaches that His judgments are righteous *in all* He does. "Foolish men contend with God in many ways as though they held him liable to their accusations...For his will is, and rightly ought to be, the cause of all things that are...when, therefore, one asks why God has so done, we must reply. Because he has willed it." God is righteous in His execution of His will and disposal of men. He cannot be charged with unreasonable actions. He is the judge who by His omniscience and wisdom executes all things by the counsel of a righteous, holy and perfect will.

Calvin does not believe God blesses (*i.e.* give a saving eye to...) the seed of the serpent. He saw children of wrath as just that, "children *of wrath.*" Until working

---

[62] Ibid, Volume 2, 947. (3.22.11)

mercy is endowed upon them, they continue in a state of curse and darkness. If they are reprobate, they are *never* delivered. Instead, their reprobation is compounded by aggravating sin they continue to commit. Calvin explains what it means to be without grace, "he [man] is so banished from the Kingdom of God that all qualities belonging to the blessed life of the soul have been extinguished in him, until he recovers them through the grace of regeneration." This does not mean man is a brute and unthinking creature. Calvin does say that the light of reason sparks within the degenerate mind of man and enables him to think about nature and about God. But it is wholly corrupted. He describes man as, "perpetually blind," "vain," "dull," "stumbling repeatedly," "grievously laboring," and "groping along in the dark."[63] He then parrots Ecclesiastes to sum up the life of men as, "vanity." How then *could* they be blessed? Calvin says that God wills good to those that are believers, but to the wicked, judgment. "But as the Lord, in testifying his benevolence toward believers by present good things, then foreshadowed spiritual happiness by such types and symbols, so on the other hand he gave, in physical

---

[63] Ibid, Volume 1, 271. (2.2.12)

punishments, proofs of his coming judgment against the wicked. Thus, as God's benefits were more conspicuous in earthly things, so also were his punishments...why...imagine different gods for the Old and New Testaments, like the Manichees!"[64]

Calvin did not believe that God gave saving grace to all men – if that were so, we would deem it *common*, and we know *grace is not common*. He says, "For I do not tarry over those fanatics who babble that grace is equally and indiscriminately distributed."[65] Calvin says that it is the "fanatics" that believe God is gracious to all men. The doctrines of God's electing grace are solely for the elect. There is no other grace outside of Jesus Christ. Thus, there is no grace for those outside of Jesus Christ. God simply renders them inexcusable when they hear the Gospel and further hardens them. Calvin says, God renders them "inexcusable." God

---

[64] Ibid, Volume 1, 452. (2.11.3)

[65] Ibid, Volume 1, 262-263. The footnote here is also worthy to note, "In his response (June 5, 1555) to questions addressed to him by Laelius Socinus (to whom he may be alluding here), Calvin distinguishes between the effective giving of grace to the elect and the "inferior operation of the Spirit" in the reprobate." It is to Hebrews 6 and 10 that Calvin would be alluding to here. The reprobate may receive some operations of the Spirit (tasting the heavenly gift, etc.) but not be saved. Yet this is not grace. God will use their hearty rejection of His Spirit to ultimately condemn them to a greater degree."

purposely gives them a confused awareness of grace, but does not show Himself merciful. Only the elect receive God's true gift of faith.[66]

Calvin believed that God was not gracious to the reprobate, but did believe God used various "good" things to further harden them, especially using the Word of God. Calvin explains Augustine's position and subsequently his own, "Augustine himself in the *Against Julian, Book V*, argues at great length that sins happen not only by God's permission and forbearance, but by His might, as a kind of punishment for sins previously committed."[67] Sins come by use of excess and violation against the law of God. A car, a house, a boat, a job, *etc.*, are all things God gives wicked men, but for the occasions of their sin. They attempt to enjoy these good things, but in reality true joy is only found *in* God. The reprobate have none of the Spirit and so use and abuse the good things God gives them for that occasion. Calvin says, "When the Spirit is taken away our hearts harden into stones." God wills to harden men in this way. He keeps the operations of the Spirit from effecting their heart and they continue to become

---

[66] Ibid, 555, Volume 1. (3.2.11)
[67] Ibid, 311. (2.4.3)

harder.[68] Calvin gives these examples, "He takes away speech from the truthful, and deprives the elders of reason (Job 12:20; cf. Ezek. 7:26). He takes the heart from those who are in authority over the people of the land, and makes them wander in trackless wastes (Job 12:24; cf. Psalm 107:40). Likewise, "O Lord why hast thou driven us mad and hardened our heart, that we may not fear thee?" (Isa. 63:17; *cf.* Vulgate.) These passages indicate what sort of men God makes..."[69] Calvin then makes an allusion to Pharaoh and then quotes Augustine, "Did he harden it by not softening it? This is indeed true, but he did something more. He turned Pharaoh over to Satan to be confirmed in the obstinacy of his breast...In another place Augustine well defines the matter, "The fact that men sin is their own doing; that they by sinning do this or that comes

---

[68] It is worthy to note that unregenerate men can "taste" (Hebrews 6, 10) the Holy Spirit, "prophesy" (King Saul) by the Holy Spirit, and other sundry operations. This does not mean they are filled or indwelt by the Holy Spirit. Hebrews 6 makes the distinction later in the chapter between those who "taste" and those who are truly saved when he distinguishes them by the phrase "things accompanying salvation."

[69] Ibid, 312. (2.4.4)

from the power of God, who divides the darkness as he pleases."[70]

In the exhortations of the Gospel men are hardened by God. "Now since promises are offered to believers and impious alike, they have their usefulness for both groups. As God by his precepts pricks the consciences of the impious in order that they, oblivious to his judgments, may not too sweetly delight in their sins..."[71] The wicked are irritated by the promises because it does not allow them to rest easy in their sin. It begins to prick and sear the conscience upon their hearing and they become harder and harder against it. This is seen more prominently in Calvin's *Book 3*, where he says, "The invitation is equal in preaching, but held out as the savor of death to the wicked."[72] which show the special and effectual calling of the elect, and the outward calling of the wicked. Here we see both senses enacted in preaching. Calvin says in this section (3.24.8) that God gives the Gospel to them as an occasion of a more severe condemnation. This is what he deemed as the "outward" call which is the form, as

[70] Ibid, 313. (2.4.5) Calvin's quote on Augustine can be found in *Nicene and Post Nicene Fathers, Volume 5*, 514, On the Predestination of the Saints.
[71] Ibid, 328. (2.5.10)
[72] Ibid, Volume 2. 974. (3.24.8)

compared to the "inward" call which was the substance or material of the Gospel. The outward call simply hardens the wicked more and more being a savor of death to them. Calvin is so blunt about the Spirit's operation here that he says, "Yet sometimes he also causes those whom he illumines only for a time to partake of it; then he justly forsakes them on account of their ungratefulness and strikes them with even greater blindness."[73] Calvin believed God deals specifically with the reprobate to harden them. He believed God dealt with them in this way, "What of those, then, whom he created for dishonor in life and destruction in death, to become the instruments of his wrath and examples of his severity? That they may come to their end, he sometimes deprives them of the capacity to hear his word; at other times he, rather, blinds and stuns them by the preaching of it...The supreme Judge, then, makes way for his predestination when he leaves in blindness those whom he has once condemned and deprived of participation in his light."[74] He also says, "That the Lord sent his Word to many whose blindness tends to increase, indeed cannot be called into question...observe that he directs his voice to them but

---

[73] Ibid.
[74] Ibid, 978-979, (3.24.12)

in order that they may become even more blind; he sets forth doctrine but that they may grow even more stupid; he employs a remedy but so they may not be healed."[75]

Calvin enjoyed Augustine thoroughly because their doctrine on the key subjects of the Bible were so closely intertwined, especially on election and reprobation. Augustine is quoted by Calvin to continue the onslaught against those who believe that God desires all men to be saved. In this next quote, we see the reformer agreeing with the early father on what may constitute the true *mystery box* for the reprobate. It is certainly not the contradictory notion that God has two wills, one to harden the reprobate and one to desire his salvation. But that God's ways concerning why he does not save all is the focus. He quotes him saying, "Therefore let us not be ashamed to say with Augustine: "God could", he says, "turn the will of evil men to good because he is almighty. Obviously he could. Why, then, does he not? Because, he wills otherwise. Why he wills otherwise rests with him."[76]

---

[75] Ibid, 980. (3.24.13)
[76] Ibid, 979. (3.24.13)

Why does God harden these men? Calvin gives the answer, "The fact that the reprobate do not obey God's Word when it is made known to them will be justly charged against the malice and depravity of their hearts, provided it be added at the same time that they have been given over to this depravity because they have been raised up by the just but inscrutable judgment of God to *show forth his glory in their condemnation.*"[77] God glorifies Himself in the reprobation of the wicked, thus, He must harden some men and eternally damn them for this glorification to come to pass. It is not that God becomes more glorious in their damnation, but that the glory of His justice is reflected by the due wrath poured out on the wicked as they continue in eternal misery. Even in the hardening of the reprobate, God is glorified exceedingly. There are more lost than there are saved ("Many are called but few are chosen..."), His justice is all the more glorified and expressed as righteous and true. In seeing this, Calvin spends a great deal of time dealing with the will of God in the compound sense (by accommodation) on this subject.

---

[77] Ibid, 981. (3.24.14) (Emphasis Mine.)

CALVIN AND NATURAL REVELATION

Before looking at Calvin's view of the Gospel call, one should take a moment and touch upon his view of natural revelation. Is there saving merit, or steps to salvation, found in the light of nature? Does Calvin believe that this is so? No he does not. Calvin did not believe that Romans 2:4 ("...the goodness of God leads you to repentance") meant that good things enabled men to repent. He said this, "If we seek God's fatherly mercy and kindly heart, we should turn our eyes to Christ, on whom alone God's Spirit rests."[78] It would be enough here to say, "Case closed." But to cut him off so quickly would be unfair. "If we seek salvation, life, and the immortality of the heavenly kingdom, then there is no other to whom we may flee, seeing that he alone is the fountain of life, the anchor of salvation, and heir of the Kingdom of Heaven...Accordingly, those whom God has adopted as his sons are said to have been chosen not in themselves but in his Christ (Eph. 1:4). For unless he could love them in him, he could not honor them with the

---

[78] Ibid, 970. (3.24.5)

inheritance of his Kingdom if they had not previously become partakers of him...Christ, then, is the mirror wherein we must, and without self-deception may, contemplate our own election...Therefore, if we desire to know whether God cares for our salvation, let us inquire whether he has entrusted us to Christ."[79] Christ is the only place any man can find saving grace. It is not found in a rock or a tree. It is not found in a car or in a bird. It is found solely in God's Son. Not even the law itself can save, but only condemns. One cannot milk salvation out of Romans 2:4 any more than one could get oil from a rock, as Calvin says.

The blessings of the Spirit of God are only given to men when they are regenerated. They do not obtain any measure of grace unless they are regenerated and have been given saving faith. Regeneration does not come through natural revelation but by the sovereign operation of the Spirit. Calvin states, "Both repentance and forgiveness of sins—that is, newness of life and free reconciliation—are conferred on us by Christ, and both are attained by us through faith...Repentance is a singular gift of God I believe to be so clear...that there is no need of a long discourse to explain it...whomsoever

---

[79] Ibid, 970-971. (3.24.5-6)

God wills to snatch from death, he quickens by the Spirit of regeneration."[80] Calvin does not place the salvation of men in rocks and trees, but in Christ alone, in the Beloved. He does not think that natural revelation saves.[81]

---

[80] Ibid, Volume 1, 592 and 615 (3.3.1; 3.3.21). Calvin also says on 615, "Indeed, God declares that he wills the conversion of all, and he directs exhortations to all in common." But this is not speaking about God's eternal decree but His perceptive will, or the divided sense of the Gospel. I do not believe Calvin here thinks that God's will is double. He may be using the words here carelessly. I think the word to remember here is "declares" which speaks of the Gospel being sent out, not effectuated.

[81] See also 1.3.1; 1.6.1 where he titles the section, "*Scripture is needed as Guide and Teacher for anyone who would come to God as Creator.* <u>God bestows the actual knowledge of Himself upon us only in the Scriptures</u>." *Institutes*, Volume 1, 69.

CALVIN'S VIEW OF THE GOSPEL CALL

In Calvin's understanding of the Gospel Call, he begins with the Old Testament Law which cannot save men. Though the law cannot save, it is not without meaning. It obviously points men to the fact that they are wicked and cannot attain the level of holiness which God requires. Calvin says the Old Testament law is, "fruitless and ineffectual for us unless God, out of his free goodness, shall receive us without looking at our works"[82] but looking at the elect through the lens of His Son. If God intervenes with the Gospel, then men will be saved. If He leaves men to the law, they will be lost. God must intervene for salvation. But mere exhortations to repent are useless. What does this mean? Is this statement referring to the Old Testament or New Testament? It refers to both. In either the Old Testament or New Testament God must intervene even if the Gospel is preached in order for men to attain salvation. This is what Calvin believed. He said, "The promises also that are offered us in the law would all be ineffectual and void, had God's goodness not helped us

---

[82] Ibid, *Volume 1*, 352. (2.7.4)

through the Gospel."[83] God's real goodness to men is seen in the Gospel, in the effectual working of the Gospel to save "sinners", as Calvin said.

Since we know that men cannot be saved, except by Christ and except by the Gospel *when made effectual by the Spirit*, Calvin spent considerable time explaining the call of the Gospel. Calvin said that the preaching of the Word is debased when presented as effectually profitable to all since there is a blurring between the external call and the internal call. "Hence it is clear that the doctrine of salvation, which is said to be reserved solely and individually for the sons of the church, is falsely debased when presented as effectually profitable to all."[84] If this is the case, then who is the call of the Gospel for if not for all? Calvin does refer to the Gospel as a "command" for men to repent, believe and come to him, but he says, "when we exhort and preach to those endowed with ears, they willingly obey, but those who lack them have fulfilled what is written: "Hearing they hear not (Isaiah 6:9)."[85] Preaching is for those who can hear.

---

[83] Ibid, 804. (3.17.2)
[84] Ibid, *Volume 2*, 944. (3.22.10)
[85] Ibid, 962. (3.23.13)

Calvin knew the universality of the promises do not make all mankind equal. If God prescribes the duty of men in the Bible (repent or perish), this in no way infers that there has been a decree by Him that wills their salvation. Preaching is shared between the elect and reprobate, they both hear the perceptive will of God; but both are not saved. Calvin called preaching a "free call." He says, "Even though the preaching of the Gospel streams forth from the wellspring of election, because such preaching is shared also with the wicked, it cannot of itself be a full proof of election. But God effectively teaches his elect that he may lead them to faith."[86] The elect are taught of God, they are the regenerate elect; they have ears to hear. But the wicked do not have ears, and with Gospel preaching they derive no profit from it. Calvin says, "God is said to have ordained from eternity those whom he wills to embrace in love, and those upon whom he wills to vent his wrath. Yet he announces salvation to all men indiscriminately. I maintain that these statements agree perfectly with each other. For by so promising He merely means that His mercy is extended to all, provided they seek after it and implore it. But only

---

[86] Ibid, *Volume 2*, 965. (3.24.1)

those He has illumined do this. And he illumines those he has predestined to salvation. These latter possess the sure and unbroken truth of the promises, so that one cannot speak of any disagreement between God's eternal election and the testimony of his grace that he offers to believers."[87]

Calvin only mentions Ezekiel 18:23 in 4.1.25 and does not expound it. But in 3.24.15 he deals with Ezekiel 33:11 (...desire not the death of the wicked...). Systematically, this is what Calvin taught on the passage: 1) Men often violently twist the will of God here applying it to a false understanding of God's desire and intention. 2) He asks the question "why does God, then, not save all?, 3) Hope of pardon is to the penitent only, which is the teaching of the passage, 4) He does not act deceitfully with the wicked, but renders them inexcusable, 5) The meaning of the passage is ultimately directed to the effectual call in believers, and 6) God's mercy and repentance are always linked together. I would encourage all readers of Calvin's

---

[87] Ibid, 985. (3.24.17) A difference must be remembered between our modern day use of the word "offer" and the Latin word "*offerre*" which means to "present or set forth" without substance in the preaching itself. The substance derives from the application of the promise by the Spirit. This is Calvin's meaning of the word, as the other Protestant Confessions, reformers, and puritans.

commentaries on Ezekiel 18:23 to read this section of the *Institutes* since this is Calvin's full mind on the subject, and the passages between the two in Ezekiel are almost identical.[88]

---

[88] Ibid, 982-983. (3.24.15) See also 983-984ff for treatments of similar "difficult" passages which men also "twist" such as 1 Timothy 2:3-4, and 2 Peter 3:9.

CALVIN'S COMMON GRACE

Calvin never uses the term "common grace" in his writings, though the idea is present. Berkhof mentions this when speaking on common grace. He says, "The name "common grace" as a designation of the grace now under discussion cannot be said to have its origin to Calvin. Dr. H. Kuiper, in his work *Calvin on Common Grace* says, that he found only four passages in Calvin's works in which the adjective "common" is used with the noun "grace," and in two of these the Reformer is speaking of saving grace."[89] It seems his understanding of "common" grace comes from the goodness of God contemplated in his "fatherly kindness" towards creation. Of all the terms Calvin employs, the designation which seems to appear most is "fatherly kindness." It is a careless statement to say that God is a *father* to wicked men. Does he mean God is Creator? When Christ speaks of His Father, he uses the term in a radically different way. Christ's Father is the personal loving Father which Christians ought to pray before as their own (Matthew 6:9ff) Calvin, though,

---

[89] Berkhof, Louis, *Systematic Theology*, (Grand Rapids: Eerdman's Publishing Co., 1988), 434.

seems to have the idea that God as "father" in this sense, "Consequently, too, there comes in that which Paul quotes from Aratus, that we are God's offspring [Acts 17:28], because by adorning us with such great excellence, he testifies that he is our Father. In the same way secular poets, out of a common feeling and, as it were, at the dictation of experience, called him "the Father of men."[90] The secular poets call God *father* in a Creator/creature distinction. But Calvin uses the term much more graphically, "Similarly, what great occasion he gives us to contemplate his mercy when he often pursues miserable sinners with unwearied kindness, until he shatters their wickedness by imparting benefits and by recalling them to him with more than fatherly kindness!"[91] He stretches the idea of God's fatherly kindness from the time of creation even until now, "But we ought in the very order of things diligently to contemplate God's fatherly love toward mankind in that he did not create Adam until he had lavished upon the universe all manner of good things."[92]

---

[90] Calvin, John, *Institutes of the Christian Religion*, Volume 1, John T. McNeil, Editor, (Philadelphia: The Westminster Press, 1960), 55.
[91] Ibid, 60.
[92] Ibid, 161-162.

Though Calvin believes God is a "father" to all men, he does make it evident that this fatherly kindness does not save men. "For even if God wills to manifest his fatherly favor to us in many ways, yet we cannot by contemplating the universe infer that he *is father*."[93] Calvin says here that God is a father to all men, but he is a hidden Father. Their depravity hinders them from knowing Him as the Father He has been all along to them in bestowing gifts upon them.

Calvin did believe that there was such a theological idea such as *general grace*. This general grace was a result of God's goodness. It also entailed some type of God's mercy, "This very might lead us to ponder his eternity; for he from whom all things draw their origin must be eternal and have beginning from himself. Furthermore, if the cause is sought by which he was led once to create all these things, and now is moved to preserve them, we shall find that it is his goodness alone. But this being the sole cause, as much as there is no creature, as the prophet declares, upon whom God's mercy has not been poured out."[94] This grace, mercy and goodness was part of his understanding of God's

---

[93] Ibid, 341, (Emphasis Mine)
[94] Ibid, 59.

complete providence. "Finally, it [providence] strives to the end that God may reveal his concern for the whole human race."[95] God is concerned with all men as a father should be. He has endowed men with the natural ability to think, which shows His goodness to them. Calvin says, "Since reason, therefore, by which man distinguishes between good and evil, and by which he understands and judges, is a natural gift, it could not be completely wiped out."[96] He also says, "Now because some are born fools or stupid, that defect does not obscure the general grace of God."[97] Calvin will even go so far to say that God restrains sin by a "type of grace" in depraved men. "But to here it ought to occur to us that amid this corruption of nature there is some place for God's grace; not such grace as to cleanse it, but to restrain it inwardly."[98] He sees God's work in the lives of men as so particular in these ways that he believes that some gifts, are not common to all, but peculiar to men, "There are not common gifts of nature, but special graces of God, which he bestows variously and in a

---

[95] Ibid, 210.
[96] Ibid, 270.
[97] Ibid, 273.
[98] Ibid 292.

certain measure upon men otherwise wicked." These would be the Mozarts and the Michelangelos.

Calvin believed that when this fatherly love is expressed, then society is better for it, though on the final Day of Judgment, it will have done men no good except to bring them to judgment. He says, "As for the virtues that deceive us with their vain show, they shall have praise in their political assembly and in common renown among men; but before the heavenly judgment seat they shall be of no value to acquire righteousness."[99] The same can be said of the gifts of painting, dancing, etc. Calvin did not believe men could be saved by them or did any good to those who had them in a saving manner, though they be bestowed by general grace, "But because sculpture and painting are gifts of God, I seek a pure and legitimate use of each, lest those things which the Lord conferred upon us for his glory and our good be not only polluted by perverse misuse but also turned to our destruction."[100]

This writer disagrees with Calvin in his use of terms. The Bible does not ascribe "*fatherly* kindness" to anyone but the Christian. The Christian has a Father

---

[99] Ibid, 294.
[100] Ibid, 59.

who is God, and the wicked have their father, the devil (John 8:44). To say that the impartation of tomatoes, cars, houses, or the ability to paint is a kind of mercy or grace of God's *Fatherly* kindness is to blur the lines between the saved and the lost tremendously. It cannot be denied that these good gifts are given to men. But to move as far as Calvin has done in these terms of general grace or fatherly kindness, is to move further than the text will allow exegetes to actually move. It would be more helpful to say "God's *Creator* Kindness."

Many times God's providence in the lives of men is referred to as general grace to men, or some kind of grace. It would have been better if Calvin defined what he meant more than he did. Though one can tell that this general grace and mercy does them no good, it would have been more helpful if Calvin stated *what it does do?* According to 1 Thess. 2:16 these things fill up the measure of men's sins as Calvin already expressed; and it leaves them inexcusable. But how then could there be another kind of grace outside of Christ, or another kind of fatherly love which really does nothing for the wicked except damn them more? How could this in any real sense be called grace?

Calvin does not need to prove to me that wicked men received good things from God, who is good. However, this does not argue God's communication of goodness to them formally. Calvin is right when he says that this general grace does not do men any good. If this is the case why is the point belabored? Calvin's idea of common or general grace is faulty because he does not explain what he means when he uses the ideas surrounding accommodation. Instead, he expects his reader to have already understood accommodation, where the reader would not. In this way Calvin had presumptively set forth a correct doctrine, but in a wrong manner.

CONCLUSION

From this short survey of the *Institutes* Calvin is on the same track that Augustine was on, and for the most part, he is likeminded with the other reformers. Some theologians appeal to the "wise and more mature Calvin" in his later years as he wrote the commentaries of John and Ezekiel for defense of their dual position of God's will. But they must remember Calvin's own words from his preface. That he was being brief in his commentaries, and would direct all those who want to know his mind concerning the Bible to look in the "conveniently" laid out *Institutes*. The *Institutes* do not show a dual will in God, or contradictory wills. To quote Calvin in his brief commentaries and not reconcile those passages with the *Institutes* is to do injustice to the reformer.

As for his view of common grace, this writer disagrees with his use of terms. Fatherly kindness cannot be ascribed to God in the way Calvin formulates it. God is only Father to His elect-redeemed, not the seed of the serpent. Calvin does attempt to portray God's love in a gleaming light, but to the distortion of the use of terms and his ideas surrounding "presumptuous" accommodation on behalf of his readers.

A NOTE ON CALVIN'S TREATISE

The following articles (in the following chapters) were initially written by Sebastian Castellio (1515-1563), who was a Frenchmen that had an initial affinity to Calvin, but later turned on him from a number of angles. Calvin replied to each of these articles in order to set down a comprehensive rebuttal, as much as Calvin thought Castellio deserved. (A history of Castellio can be found in Hans R. Guggisberg's work, *Sebastian Castellio 1515–1563, Humanist and Defender of Religious Toleration in a Confessional Age*.)[101] This work was later known and published by Calvin as, "Concerning the Secret Providence of God," (1558) and is taken mostly in the warping of Calvin's views of the reprobation of the wicked.

Castellio had spent much time with Calvin, living in his house, as well as attempting to gain his reputation in a work he wanted to complete in translating the Scriptures with Calvin's backing. But at

---

[101] For a more summarized treatment of a biography of Castellio, see Paul Helm's introduction to "Calvin's Secret Providence of God," by Crossway books.

every turn, Castellio was a disappointment. Instead of furthering reform, he was a hindrance to it, and he turned on Calvin in a rigorous manner. He wrote against Augustinianism, against Reformed orthodoxy, against the expulsion of heretics, and personally attacked the Genevan council in writing against the death of Servetus. This all culminated with an attack on Calvin's view of reprobation and providence (in a larger scope than we traditionally think of today) and was first circulated around 1557. He wrote the work anonymously, as he did with Servetus' document.[102]

Castellio's work was a list of 14 articles he gleaned from various sections of Calvin's work, with questions and his responses. Keep in mind, Castellio's sub-par work, proof texts Calvin repeatedly and Calvin, over and over, will correct Castellio's mishandling of his work. When Calvin responded to this work, he responded point by point while quoting Castellio in full. In doing so, he not only shows Castellio's inability to understand Reformed truth, but to handle Scripture effectively.

---

[102] In writing against the Genevan Council he used a pen name instead of his own to continue some form of anonymity which didn't last long.

Castellio would put to shame most of the Arminian or Semi-Pelagian books that have been published today against the Reformation. He is far more thoughtful, and a better handler of Scripture than any of the Arminian theologians that have been published in the last 100 years, including the Arminian grandfather Pelagius and the Pelagians of yesteryear such as Charles Finney. Yet, Calvin radically dispels Castellio point by point, and demonstrates the foolishness of his work, and the inadequacy of both his understanding of Scripture or even of simple logic. The heart of every Pelagian or Arminian error runs in the same course – if God controls whatsoever comes to pass, then how can God *sincerely* command what is contrary with what he decrees *shall* come to pass? This has been the age old problem with the proof texted version of any Satanic ploy against the truth. Calvin handles this masterfully and expounds this important truth as it applies especially to reprobation. How can God require one thing in his word, and decree another? Or the reverse – whatever God has not commanded in his word, how can that be willed by God? And if there is no problem with this supposed conundrum, how do we escape the implied "dual will" in God? Does God desire all men to be saved and yet reprobate most of the people in history to hell? How do these square up against Scriptures which are so familiar as John 3:16?

In sum, Calvin will explain the conundrum, dispelling that such a conundrum exists. He will show that there is a difference between God's decree (his secret will) and his precepts (his revealed will in scripture). Though we may not understand everything we would "like" in the internal workings of such a tension, Calvin shows very plainly that God uses sin sinlessly (without doing any injustice to the will of the creature performing the sin), and decrees evil righteously (without being tainted by the sin he decrees for his ultimately glory).

CONCERNING THE SECRET PROVIDENCE OF GOD

BY JOHN CALVIN

A LETTER OF A DISSENTER TO REPROBATION AGAINST THE DOCTRINE OF JOHN CALVIN

John Calvin,

Though your name is very famous in almost *the whole world*, and your doctrine has undoubtedly many abettors, yet it has also many adversaries. Now, as it is my eager wish, that doctrine were one, a truth is one, and that all if possible might harmonize in it, I have supposed that you should be frankly informed of the objections continually made to your doctrine. And if your doctrine is false, you may refute them, and send the refutation to us, that so we may be able to withstand the gainsayers. And let your reasons be such as the people can understand.

Though there are many things in regard to which many differ with you, yet deferring other matters to another time, I shall at present handle with you, the single argument concerning fate or predestination, both because this point is exciting great tumults in the church, which we would desire to see terminated; and because in this instance, the arguments of the adversaries, cannot as yet be refuted, from the books which you have published.

I will here set down in a desultory way, certain articles taken from your books, and tossed about in this discussion. I will then subjoin what is ordinarily alleged against each article, that you may perceive what requires an answer.

JOHN CALVIN'S REPLY TO THE DISSENTER'S PREFACE

That my doctrine has many adversaries, is neither unknown nor astonishing to me. For it is no new thing for Christ, beneath whose standard I contend, to be the object of abuse to many babblers. On this account alone I grieve, that through my side is pierced the sacred and eternal truth of God, which ought to be reverently esteemed and adored by the whole world. But when I see that from the beginning, truth has been subject to the many calumnies of the wicked, and that Christ himself (for the Celestial Father has so decreed) must necessarily be the mark for contradiction, this also should be patiently endured. The virulent assaults of the wicked, however, shall never make me repent of that doctrine which I am assured has God for its author. Nor do I have so little profited by the many conflicts in which God has exercised me, that I should now be alarmed at your futile *outcry*. Besides, so far as you are privately concerned, my masked adviser, this is some consolation, that you could not be ungrateful to a man, who had obliged you more than you deserved, without at the same time betraying foul impiety against God. I know, indeed, that to you Academicians, there is no sweeter game than under color of doubt, to pluck up every particle of faith in the hearts of men. And how witty in your apprehension that raillery is, which you cast against the secret providence of God, is sufficiently evident from your style, dissemble it as you may. But I summon you and your companions to that Tribunal, where *by and by* the Celestial Judge, by the lightning alone of his face and breath, will effectually prostrate your audacity. Meanwhile, I am confident, that I can soon render your smartness as offensive to honest and wise readers, as it is secretly pleasant to yourself.

You demand of me a refutation of your treatise which you sent to Paris from Geneva, by stealth; and this was unknown to me. The poison might be scattered far and wide, without its antidote; and while you affect some desire of information, you suppress your name, for no reason that I can imagine, but because you were aware that I had something at hand, which would at once destroy the credit of you and your gang. From many marks, however, I can conjecture, no, I may conclude, who you are. But it is of no importance to me, whether you wrote with your own hand, or whether you dictated to a Scottish preacher of your frenzies, with the design of his carrying to Paris, what it was unlawful to publish here. I could wish indeed, either that this pamphlet had another author, or that you were a different man from what you are; and that you will never be until you have felt the loveliness of candor. Though in your dealings with me you were never deficient in respect, yet it was easy to see how prone you are by nature to cavil. This vice, which you aggravated by childish whims, I endeavored to correct, but in vain, because your natural tendency had been aggravated by a wretched vanity, which strained after the praise of acuteness, on the ground of a few very silly and worse than insipid jokes. Nor can you defend yourself by the example of Socrates, who was accustomed to sift by his objections, and opinions of every kind. For, while that man was illustrious, for many distinguished excellences, they were all tarnished by that vice, in which alone, you, with no less impropriety than eagerness seek to rival him.

You demand of me a refutation of your treatise, such as *the people can understand*. Now, I have here labored to accommodate myself to the apprehension of the simple, by a style of instruction, at once perspicuous and pure. But if you receive no statement as argument, except what the sense of carnal man approves, by such proud disdain, you do, with your own hand, bar the approach to that doctrine, the knowledge of which begins in reverence. Nor am I ignorant of your jibes, and those like you, with which you assail God's mysteries. This is just as if everything must lose its grace and authority, that does not strike your fancy. And what is meant by requiring me to refute everyone who shall choose to rail at me? For even Socrates, whose authority you falsely allege, would have submitted to no such rule. I for my part have no fondness for indiscriminate imitation; but if there ever was not only in this age, but in any other, a man who constantly set himself against the wicked, by dissipating their calumnies; even those who dislike and injure me, will give me some credit for that kind of industry. Wherefore your rant is more intolerable, because, while with the blind impetuosity of impudence, you trample on all my labors, you enjoin a task already three or four times accomplished.

But you maintain there is one point, on which I am defeated by my adversaries; in so far as no sufficient materials for a defense, can be found in anything which

I have here published. That point, you say, is predestination or fate. I would it had been your design, either modestly to inquire, or at least to dispute with candor, rather than by outraging all decency, and for the sake of extinguishing the light, to confound things the most opposite. Fate, according to the Stoics, is a necessity springing out of a changeable, and complicated labyrinth, and binding in some measure God himself. Instructed by the Scriptures, I define predestination, *as the free counsel of God, by which he regulates the human race, and all the individual parts of the universe, according to his own immense wisdom, and incomprehensible justice.* Now, if the depravity of your disposition, and the lust of contention, and the pride of the devil blinds you so much that you see nothing at midday, yet this distinction will demonstrate to all readers who have eyes, what fairness there is in your criticism. Besides, had you not grudged even a glance at my books, you might there have inferred, how little pleased I am with that profane word *fate*. No, you would have read that the same objection was long ago malignantly and invidiously brought against Augustine, by foul fellows, and men like yourself; and in the reply of that pious and holy doctor, there is a brief statement of what is sufficient for my defense today.

In the articles too, which you say have been extracted from my books, the case with me is the same as with that author of happy memory. As the malevolent were aware, that this doctrine was not popular, they with the design of aggravating the dislike of it, flung about passages, partly mutilated, partly distorted, so that it was impossible for the uninformed, to come to any but an unfavorable judgment. But though at first sight many supposed them extracted from his writings, yet he complains that they were falsely imputed to him; inasmuch as they had either industriously heaped together broken sentences, or by changing a few words, had artfully corrupted pious and sound doctrine, in order to create offence in the minds of the simple. That those articles which you boast of propounding from my books, are precisely of the same kind, wise and honest readers will easily discover, even though I were silent. And to such it will not be troublesome, to compare my doctrine with your foul calumnies. And this I maintain, first of all, that you act neither a manly nor an ingenious part, when you specify no passages, to show intelligent readers, that I write what you allege. For what can be more unjust, when I have published so many books, than vaguely to declare, that out of about fifty volumes, fourteen articles have been gathered? It had unquestionably been better, were a drop of honesty in you, either to quote my sentences word for word. Or if you perceived anything dangerous, to have warned your readers of what passages to beware. Whereas, by branding all my works promiscuously, you would destroy their remembrance; and what in my books might be read without any offence, you malignantly corrupt for your own convenience, and so render hateful. Now while I do not blame the prudence of Augustine, in so tempering his replies as to avoid some type of odium when he met the unprincipled craft of his adversaries, yet I think it better frankly to repel your slanders, than to give the smallest symptom of turning my back.

THE FIRST ARTICLE

God, by a simple and pure act of his will, created the greatest part of the world for destruction.

The Dissenter Against the First Article

Such is the first article; take likewise what is said against it. They say, the first article is against nature, and against Scripture. Of nature they allege this. Every animal naturally loves its offspring; now this nature is from God, from which it follows that God loves his offspring. For he would never make animals love their offspring, if *he himself* likewise did not love his. And this they prove by the following argument. The Lord hath said, "Shall I cause to bring forth, and shall I not bring forth," (Isa. 66:9). Therefore, by a parity of reason, they deduce the argument, *God makes animals love their offspring; therefore he himself loves his offspring.* But all men are the offspring of God; for God is the Father of Adam, from whom all men are sprung. *Therefore he loves all men.* But to create in order to destroy, is not the part of love, but of hatred. Therefore he created no man for destruction. Besides, creation is a work of love, not of hatred; consequently in love, not in hatred, God created all men. Moreover, there is no beast so savage, (not to speak of man,) as to design the misery of its young, in their production. How much less God? Were he not worse than even a wolf? Christ argues in this way, "If ye being evil, know how to give good gifts unto your children, how much more God?" Your adversaries also argue in this way, If Calvin though wicked, would yet be unwilling to beget a son for misery, how much less God? These and such like things they speak concerning nature.

Of Scripture on the other hand, they speak in this way, *God saw all that he had made, and it was very good;* therefore, man, whom he had made, was very good. But if God had created him for destruction, he had created a good thing for destruction, and loves to destroy what is good; which is impious even to think. Besides God created one man, to place him in paradise, which is a happy life; therefore, he created all men for a happy life. For all were created in one. And if all fell in Adam, all must have stood in Adam, and that on the same condition as Adam. Again, "I have no pleasure in the death of the wicked." Again, "[God] is not willing that any should perish; but would that all should come to the knowledge of the truth." Again, if God created the greatest part of the world for destruction, it follows that his anger must be *greater* than his mercy; and yet the Scriptures declare that he is slow to anger; so that his anger extends only to the third or fourth generation, while his mercy reaches even to the thousandth.

J. Calvin's Reply to the first article and the criticism of the Dissenter

The first article you take hold of, is, that God, by a simple and pure act of his will, created the greatest part of the world for destruction. Now, all that about, "the greatest part of the world," and, "the simple pure act of the will of God," is fictitious, and the product of the workshop of your malice. For, though God from the beginning decreed whatsoever was to come to pass with the whole human race, yet this way of talking is nowhere to be met with in my writings, that *the end of creation is eternal destruction*. Therefore like a swine, you upset with your snout, a doctrine of good odor, in order to find in it something offensive. Besides, though the will of God is to me the highest of all reasons, yet I everywhere teach that where the reason of his counsels and his works does not appear, the reason is hid with him; so that he has always decreed justly and wisely. Therefore I not only reject, I detest the trifling of the Schoolmen about absolute power, because they separate his justice from his authority. Now see, dog, what you gain by your froward barking. I, subjecting as I do the human race to the will of God, loudly declare that he decrees nothing without the best reason, which if unknown to us now, shall be cleared up at last. You, thrusting forward your, "simple and pure act of will," impudently upbraid me with that, which I openly reject in a hundred places or more. At the same time, I do acknowledge this as my doctrine, that not merely by the permission of God, but by his secret counsel also, Adam fell, and in his fall, dragged down all his descendants into *everlasting perdition*. Both assertions, as I perceive, are offensive to you, as repugnant at once to nature and Scripture. Your argument from nature is founded on the love which every animal naturally feels towards its own offspring. You therefore infer, that God who has inspired even brute beasts with this affection must love men no less, since they are his offspring. But it is too gross to insist on finding in God the author of nature, whatever you discern in the ox, and the ass, as if God were bound by the very same laws which he has given to his creatures. To secure the continuance of every race of animals, God has endowed each with the appetite of generating offspring. Now expostulate with him, why from all eternity content with himself alone, he kept his energy, as it were, barren. Undoubtedly he must be always like himself. If then, you may be judge, he violated the order of nature, so long as he chose rather to be without offspring, than to put forth his productive power. Besides, while beasts fight even to death, in behalf of their young, how is it that God allows little infants to be torn and devoured by tigers, or bears, or lions, or wolves? Is it because his arm is too short to reach forth protection to his own? You perceive how wide a field is open to me, if I cared about exposing your follies; but this alone is enough for me, that there are evidences of God's love, toward the whole human race, sufficient to convict all who perish, of ingratitude. Nor yet is this inconsistent with that peculiar love which he restricts to the few, whom he is pleased to select among many. Certainly he openly declared, by his ancient adoption of the family of Abraham, that he by no means embraces the whole human family, with equal regard. So by rejecting Esau, and preferring his younger brother Jacob, he gave an illustrious proof of that free favor, which he bestows only on *whom he pleases*. Moses proclaims that one nation had been chosen by God to the rejection of all the rest. The prophets everywhere affirm, that the only reason of the superiority of the Jews, was the unmerited favor of God. Will you deny him to be God; because in this you discover no resemblance to a tiger or a bear? It was not in vain that Christ, addressing the little flock (and not the human race, nor even indiscriminately the Jewish nation) said, "fear not, it has pleased the Father to give you the kingdom," because none but those whom he reconciles to himself, in his Only Begotten Son, experience his paternal love, in the hope of eternal life. Now, if you mean to subject God to the laws of nature, you will accuse him of injustice, in condemning us all to the penalty of eternal death, on account of the sin of one. One sinned, all are dragged to punishment; and not only so, but from the crime of one they all contract contagion, and are born corrupted and tainted with a mortal malady. Worthy critic! What have you to say to this? Will you condemn God as cruel, because he has precipitated all his offspring into ruin, for the fault of one man? For though Adam destroyed himself and his descendants, yet we must ascribe the corruption and the guilt, to the secret determination of God; because, the sin of one man were nothing to us, if the Celestial Judge did not doom us to eternal ruin on account of it.

And observe how skillfully you quote a passage of Isaiah to gloss your error. Whereas it seemed incredible that the Church of God, which in Babylonish captivity, not only was deprived of her children, but had become barren, should, with renovated vigor, be more fruitful than before, God speaks in this way, "Shall not I, by whose strength women bring forth, be able also to produce offspring?" Under this pretext, you compel God to assume all the properties of the brutes. You audaciously argue, because God makes animals love their offspring, that he too must love his offspring. Though this would be admitted, it would not follow that he loves them in the same way. Besides, this does not prove, that he may not as a just Judge reject those, whom, as the best of Fathers, he follows with affection and indulgence.

Again, you object that creation is a work of love, not of hatred; that consequently God creates from love, and not from hatred. But you do not distinguish, that though all are odious to God in Adam, yet his love shines in creation. Therefore, anyone endowed with moderate judgment, and candor, will acknowledge the frivolity of that which you fancy so plausible. What follows is not so much for me to refute with my pen, as for the magistrate severely to punish by the sword. Shall it be imputed to my books that men are undeniably born to misery? How does it come that we are exposed not merely to temporal miseries, but also to eternal death, if not because God has cast us into a common condemnation on account of the sin of one man? In this miserable ruin of the human race, it is not my opinion that is read, but God's manifest work that is beheld. You, with no misgiving, vomit the impious declaration that God is worse than any wolf, if he resolves to create men for misery. Some are born blind, others deaf, and some are prodigiously deformed. If you, indeed, may be judge, God is cruel in afflicting his offspring with such disadvantages before they come into light. But by and by, you shall feel, how much better it had been for you never to have seen at all, than to have been so perspicacious in discussing the secrets of God. You, indeed, accuse God of injustice, no, call him a *monster*, if he manages the human race in a manner different from what we do our children. Why then does he create some dull, others stupid, and others idiots? As some of the Jew's fables of the fauns and satyrs being unfinished, because their Maker was cut short by the Sabbath, will you be so absurd as to maintain that such persons slipped incomplete out of the hands of God? Such sad sights should rather teach us reverence and modesty, than produce a debate out of our brains with the Maker of heaven and earth. If I meet an idiot, I am admonished by the sight, knowing what God *might* have created me as. As many as are stupid and dull, just so many mirrors does God present, in which I may behold a power, no less awful than wonderful. But you allow yourself to rail at him as worse than a wolf, for consulting so ill for his creatures.

True, Christ declares, that God who is good, acts more kindly towards his sons, than men who are evil; but before you can turn this to your purpose, you must prove that *all* are equally the sons of God. Now, it is clear, that all lost eternal life in Adam, whereas the grace of adoption is special. Therefore, it will rather follow, that so many as are alienated from God are abhorred by him. Your texts are darts hurled at random by the hand of a madman. God saw the things which he had made, and they were very good; therefore you infer that man was very good; and again conclude, that God was unjust if he created a good being for destruction.

The nature of man's original rectitude I have sufficiently expounded, and more than sufficiently, in many passages. Doubtless he was not better than the devil, before he had fallen from his integrity. Now were I to grant you, that man, as well as apostate angels, created for happiness, and yet maintain that in respect of future defection they were destined to destruction, what will you make of it? For, undoubtedly, God knew what would happen to both and what he himself would do; he at the same time decreed it. As to permission, we shall consider it afterwards in its own place. But now if you object that the foreknowledge of God is not the cause of evil, I would only demand of you that if God foresaw the fall, both of the devil and of man before creation, why did he not by a timely precaution prevent their proneness to fall? From the beginning of the world, the devil forthwith alienated himself from the hope of salvation. Man as soon as created, overwhelmed himself and posterity in a fatal ruin. If their perseverance was in the hand of God, why did he suffer them to fall? No, why was neither furnished with even a moderate degree of constancy?

Turn as you will, I will hold this principle, that however weak and liable to fall man might be created, this weakness was very good; because his ruin was so soon to show that out of God, there was no strength, no stability. Therefore it is also evident that your prating about men being made for happiness is lame and thoughtless assertion. For though I acknowledge that there was nothing in man contrary to salvation, I prove that happiness was not predestinated for all in the secret council of God. I will briefly repeat the same thing in other words. If the natural completeness, with which man was endowed at his first creation, is alone considered, then he was made *for* happiness, inasmuch as no cause of death will there be found. If on the other hand, we inquire concerning secret predestination, we come upon that deep abyss, which should call forth instant admiration.

Besides, if you were imbued with the slightest relish for piety, you would readily acknowledge that these words, "all things were very good," were not intended to express their perfection, as if the Holy Spirit declared that nothing was needful to the excellence of any creature, but rather to cut off occasion of railing from you, and those like you.

For, however, you may deny that it was good for men to be created under this law, by which his fall was immediately to corrupt the whole world, yet God declares that this arrangement was pleasing to Himself and therefore most upright. That you may the better understand the meaning of Moses, he is not asserting how just or upright man was, but to quell your barking, he teaches that the constitution established by God in regard to man could not be surpassed in rectitude. Accordingly, although in speaking of each of God's works, he declares that God saw what he had made, and they were every one good, he does not affirm any such thing of man in particular; but to the narrative of his creation, he only adds in general, "whatever God made was very good." Under this declaration it is unquestionable, we must comprehend what Solomon teaches, that *the wicked are created for the day of evil*. The sum is this, though man by nature was good, this rectitude, which was frail and fading, was not inconsistent with the divine predestination which doomed him to perish for his own sin, who, considering merely the purity of his nature, no, the excellence with which he was adorned, had been created for happiness. And therefore you falsely and foolishly infer that he was created to perish though good, when it is manifest he fell by his own infirmity, and did not perish until he became obnoxious to a just condemnation. That these two things are mutually harmonious, we shall see more clearly later. You object that God *does not desire the death of the sinner*. But mark what follows in the prophet, the *invitation* of all to repentance. Pardon, therefore, is offered to all who return. Now, we must ascertain whether the conversion which God requires depends on every man's free will, or whether it is the *special gift* of God. In so far then, as all are invited to repent, the prophet properly denies that the death of the sinner is desired. But the reason why he does not convert all is hid with himself.

Your unoriginal quotation from Paul, that *God would have all men saved*, I have, in my judgment, elsewhere sufficiently shown, lends no countenance to your error. For it is more certain than certainty itself, that Paul is not there speaking of individuals, but refers to orders and classes of employments. He had been enjoining prayers, in behalf of kings and other governors, and all who exercised the office of magistrate. But inasmuch as all who then bore the sword were the professed enemies of the church, it might seem absurd that the church should pray for their salvation. To obviate the difficulty, Paul extends the grace of God even to them.

There is perhaps more color in the words of Peter, that, "God is not willing that any should perish, but that all should come to repentance." If, however, there is any ambiguity in the former clause, it is removed by the explanation which is immediately subjoined. Certainly in so far as God would receive all to repentance, he would have no one perish. But in order to be received, *they must come.* Now, the Spirit everywhere proclaims, that divine grace first comes to men who, *until they are drawn,* remain the willing slaves of carnal contumacy. If you had the smallest judgment remaining, would you not perceive the wide difference between these two? That the stony hearts of men, become hearts of flesh, so as to lose all self-complacency, and suppliantly entreat for pardon. Then, when they are in this way changed, that pardon is received. God declares that both these are the gifts of his kindness, the new heart for repentance, and the gracious pardon of the suppliants. Unless God were ready to receive all who truly implore his mercy, he would not say, "return unto me, and I will return unto you." But if repentance were the effect of the will of man, Paul would not say, "if peradventure God may give them repentance." No, unless the same God, who with his own voice calls all to repentance, drew his elect by the secret influences of his Spirit, Jeremiah would not say, "Turn me, Oh Lord, and I shall be turned; for when thou turnedst me, I repented."

If any modesty could be looked for in a dog, this solution should have been familiar to you from my writings as a thing ten times repeated. But, even reject it if you will, you will yet derive no more countenance from Paul, than from Ezekiel. There is no occasion for anxious debate, regarding the mode in which God would have all men saved; for these two things, salvation and the knowledge of the truth, are not to be separated. Now answer! If God determined to make known his truth to all, why since the time that the Gospel began to be proclaimed, are there so many nations that his pure truth *never reached*? Besides, why has he not equally opened the eyes of all, when the interior illumination of the Spirit, is but given to few, and is necessary to faith? This knot also you have to untie. As no one comes to God except he who is drawn by the secret influence of his Spirit, why are not all indiscriminately drawn, if he is determined that *all* should be saved? For the discrimination demonstrates, that there is some secret way, in which he excludes many from salvation.

How it is that the mercy of God reaches to the thousandth generation, you will never perceive while you are blinded by the pride which puffs you up. For there is no promise of such a mercy, as was to abolish utterly the curse, under which the whole progeny of Adam was overwhelmed. But the mercy promised was to make its way forever to the unworthy in spite of all the obstacles which might oppose. In this way God passed by many sons of Abraham when he chose Isaac alone. So when Isaac had begotten twins, the same God determined that he should rest only on Jacob.

God gives proof of his anger against many; still this remains undeniable, that he is inclined to goodness, slow to anger, because in the long suffering with which he tolerates the reprobate, there is no obscure display of his goodness.

Now observe how your frivolous quibbles entangle yourself while I escape with such ease. That the mercy of God may exceed his anger, you insist that more must be chosen to salvation than destruction;

now though I were to grant this, yet God will be unjust to those few, if your calumnies may be believed. If he does not love his offspring you pronounce him worse than a wolf. If then there is but one against whom he exercises his anger, how will he escape the charge of cruelty? Nor may you object, that the causes of anger are in men themselves; because comparing anger with mercy, you contend merely concerning relative extent; as if by choosing more to salvation, God might prove himself merciful. Whereas God commends his love toward us in a totally different way, viz on the one hand, by pardoning so many, and so various offences, and on the other by contending with the obstinate malice of men, until it comes to its height.

THE SECOND ARTICLE

God not only predestinated to damnation; but he also predestinated Adam to the causes of damnation; whose fall he not only foresaw, but determined from eternity by a secret decree, and ordained that he should fall. And that this might come to pass in his time, he set forth the apple the cause of the fall.

The Dissenter against the Second Article

They say that the second too is a doctrine of the devil, and they demand of us, Calvin, to show where it is written in the word of God.

Calvin's Reply

In the second article you are the same man still. Produce the passage from my writings, where I teach that the apple was set before Adam to cause his fall. This to be sure is one of your popular arts, to darken the minds of the simple with lies, lest they should rise to the truth, which is remote from common carnal sense. But lest I should seem to dispute about words, I acknowledge that I wrote in this way – *that the fall of*

Adam was not a matter of chance, but ordained in the secret counsel of God. In simply denouncing this a doctrine of the devil, you must no doubt fancy yourself a judge of no mean authority. Otherwise, you could not expect to overturn with one abusive assertion, a point which I have established by powerful arguments. You demand a testimony from Scripture to demonstrate that Adam did not fall without the secret decree of God. Whereas, if you had only read a few pages with attention, you could not help seeing what is everywhere obvious, that God manages all things according to his secret counsel. You fancy a foreknowledge in God, which sluggishly beholds from heaven the life of man. God himself, laying his hand on the helm of the universe, does not allow his power to be separated from his foreknowledge. Certainly this reasoning belongs to *Augustine*, not to me. If God foresaw what he was unwilling should happen, then he is not supreme. Therefore he determined whatever should be, because independently of his will, nothing could be. If you reckon this as absurd, yet you cannot escape it even with your fancy; because he ought to have at least applied to the mischief the remedy within his own power though it is clear he did not do so. God foresaw the fall of Adam. He had the power of preventing it. He was not willing to prevent it. Why he was unwilling no reason can be given, except that his will took the opposite direction. If you allow yourself to contend with God, then accuse him too of fitting man for ruin, by the weakness in which he created him. You say that *Adam fell by free will.* I reply that to keep him from falling, he needed that constancy and fortitude with which God endows his elect when he determines that they shall hold fast their integrity. It is sure, unless new strength is supplied from heaven every moment, we are frail enough to perish a thousand times. God supports those whom he has chosen, and they persevere with invincible fortitude. Why should he not have supplied Adam with this, if he willed him to stand unhurt? Surely we must here be silent, or confess with Solomon that God made all things for himself, *even the wicked for the day of evil.* If the absurdity offends you, think that this is not some vain repetition which declares the judgments of God to be a great deep. If the incomprehensible counsel of God could be contained in the little measure of our capacity, it was in vain that Moses proclaimed that the revelations of the Law were *for us and our children,* while *his secret things* belonged to himself. You demand a quotation proving that God did not prevent the fall of Adam, because he was unwilling; as if indeed the memorable answer did not sufficiently prove it, "I will have mercy on whom I will have mercy." Therefore Paul infers that he does not have mercy on all because he does not choose. And doubtless without any commentator at all, the words plainly tell us, that God is bound by no law, to show indiscriminate mercy to all. But that he is his own Arbiter in pardoning whom he pleases, and passing by others. Surely it was the same God, of whom the prophet asserts, "he doeth according to his will." Now if you say that he unwillingly yielded, when Adam fell, you must suppose that Satan was victorious in the contest, and like the Manicheans, you will have two principles. Paul too handling this subject, does not rashly compare God to the potter who was at liberty out of the same mass to make whatever variety of vessels he thought proper. The Apostle certainly might have begun at sin, though he does not, but defends the unconstrained right and sovereignty of God, in the work itself. And when he adds that all had been *shut up in unbelief*, does he teach that this happened in spite of God, or rather that God was the author of it? If you object that all were condemned for unbelief, merely because they deserved it, the context is against you, because Paul is discoursing of the secret judgments of God; and the exclamation, "O the depth," *etc.*, is inconsistent with such a supposition.

Therefore, as Christ was predestinated from the beginning to succor the lost, so God determined in his own incomprehensible counsel how he was to illustrate his own glory by the fall of Adam. I acknowledge, indeed, when he vindicates the free course of his mercy, he speaks of the human race, as it had already perished in Adam; but the same reason was always valid before the fall of Adam, that his own will is to him a sufficient ground of mercy, when such is his pleasure. This will, moreover, though it depends on nothing else, and has no more cause, is yet founded in the best reason and the highest equity. For though the license of man requires the bridle of the Law, it is otherwise with God, who is a law to himself, and whose will is the rule of the most perfect righteousness.

THE THIRD ARTICLE

The sins which are committed, are committed not only by the permission, but also by the will of God. For it is frivolous to make a distinction between the permission and the will of God, so far as sin is concerned. Those who do so wish to gain God's favor by compliments and adulation.

The Dissenter against the Third Article

Against the third, concerning the difference between will and permission, they allege this. Calvin says, that he is a prophet of God, and we say that Calvin is a prophet of the devil. Now, one of us must be saying what is false. For if he is a prophet of God, we lie; but if he is a prophet of the devil, he himself lies in saying that he is a prophet of God. But if both of these are by the will of God, that is, if God wills that Calvin should say he is a prophet of God, and that we should say, he is the prophet of the devil, he wills incompatible things which is impossible. Or if God wills a lie, he does not will the truth, or if he wills truth he does not will a lie. Therefore it follows, if he wishes one party to speak truth, he is unwilling that the other should lie.

But one or other of the parties undoubtedly lies, it lies, therefore, not by the will, but by the permission of God. There is then a difference even in God between permission and volition.

They also bring forward many clear examples, of the difference between volition and permission; especially from the twentieth chapter of Ezekiel where God after largely upbraiding his people for their unwillingness to obey his precepts at last concludes this, "go ye, serve everyone his filthy god, since ye obey not me." As if he said this, *I permit you to follow your own lust, since ye will not obey my precepts.* And this seems to be the same, as he had spoken before in the same chapter, "As they rejected my laws, I delivered to them precepts not good." Now God did not give the Israelites precepts that were not good; for all God's precepts are good. But because they rejected God's good precepts, he deserted them; and they deserted by God fell into bad precepts; just as the prodigal son, when deserted by his father, or rather when his father was deserted, fell into wantonness; and as Paul teaches, because men did not love the truth, God sent them a spirit of error to believe a lie.

Such seems to be the idea also of that passage in the fourth chapter of Amos, "Go to Bethel and sin, since ye love to do it." So now, as men are unwilling to obey God, who declares that he does not will sin, God has permitted spirits of error to exist, who teach that God wills sin; that those who are unwilling to obey the truth, may obey a lie.

They also bring forward the passage from Zechariah, where God declares himself angry with the nations that were at rest; because when he was slightly incensed against the Israelites, the heathens aggravated the punishment; that is, they more grievously vexed the Israelites, than the anger of God could tolerate; therefore, it was by the permission, not by the will of God.

They adduce a similar instance from the Prophet Obadiah, who reproves the Israelites, for afflicting the Jews, more grievously than the anger of God demanded. They also refer to the example of the prodigal son, which I have already touched on. If you say that he ran his vicious course by the will of his father, it would be most absurd; it was then by his permission. So, the guilty, they say, are the prodigal children of God, and sin by the permission, not by the will of God. Also that saying of Christ, "Will ye also go away?" Certainly he was unwilling that they should go away, but he permitted it. Finally they appeal to common sense, which dictates a difference between volition and permission, according to which, common sense Christ was accustomed to teach divine things, and which if you subvert, all the parables of Christ must perish, because common sense alone can judge of them.

Calvin's Reply

The third article no less than the others, betrays your extreme fondness, for odious calumnies. If you will attack my doctrine, why not at least show candor enough to quote my own language? In our present discussion, I maintain the distinction between permission and volition to be *frivolous*. You oppose what you fancy a witty subtlety, but what is really a silly sophism, viz., if God wills all things, he wills incompatible things, inasmuch as you call me a prophet of the devil, while I affirm myself to be a faithful servant of God. This apparent inconsistency, indeed, dazzles your eyes; but truly, God himself, who knows well how at once to will and not to will the same thing, is not concerned about your dimness of sight. Whenever God raised up true prophets, he certainly willed that they should actively and strenuously contend, in maintaining the doctrine of his law; false prophets arose who labored to subvert that doctrine. There must be a conflict between them; but God did not conflict with himself when he raised up both. You here thrust the divine toleration in my face; while he openly proclaims (Deut. 13:1), that no false prophets arise, whom he does not ordain, either to try the faith of his own, or to blind the unbelieving. "If a false prophet shall arise among you," says Moses, "your God tries you." You, by a most impertinent commentary, transfer to a totally different quarter, what Moses ascribes, not rashly to God. Either deny that it is the prerogative of God to examine the hearts of his people, or yield at length to the clear and indubitable truth, that false prophets, are God's instruments in that examination of which he chooses to be recognized as the author.

Ezekiel (14:9) is still clearer, "if a deceived prophet has brought forth anything, I God have deceived that prophet, and my hand is upon him." You enjoin us to be content with mere permission. God declares his own will and hand to be at work. Now mark, which witness is better entitled to belief: God speaking of himself by his Spirit, the only fountain of wisdom, or you prating of his unknown mysteries, according to your carnal silly apprehension? What? When God calls Satan as the executioner of his vengeance, and openly commissions him to deceive, does this differ in no respect from a simple permission? The voice of God (1 Kings 22:20-21,) is distinct enough, "who for us *will deceive* Ahab?" And there is no obscurity in the command given to Satan, "Go and be a lying spirit in the mouth of all his prophets."

I would also know whether doing and permitting are the same thing. Because David had secretly abused his neighbor's wife, God (2 Sam. 12:11), declares, that he will bring it about, that his wives shall be dragged to similar infamy, in the sight of the sun. He does not say *I will allow it to be done*, but *I will do it*. You, to aid him with your hollow help, plead permission as an apology. David himself was of a very different mind, who, reflecting on the dreadful judgment of God, exclaims, "I am dumb because thou didst it." So also, when Job blesses God, he does not merely acknowledge that by the divine permission, he had been spoiled by the robbers, but distinctly affirms that God had taken away what he had given.

If the same rule holds in giving and receiving, then by your authority, wealth cannot be a gift of God; but must flow to us casually by the divine permission. Now, though you with your corrupt crew, do not cease to rail, yet God will justify himself. But we will reverently adore mysteries, which far transcend our comprehension, until a full knowledge of them shine forth, when, face to face, we shall behold Him who now can be discerned only as in a glass. Then, Augustine says, shall be seen in the clearest light of wisdom, what the faith of the pious holds, how certain, and immutable, and most efficacious is the will of God. How many things it could do, but chooses not to do while it chooses nothing to which it is unequal. But from the lips of the same pious writer, I answer you on the point at hand. "These are the great works of the Lord, immaculate in respect of all his volitions, and so wisely immaculate, that when the angelic and human creature had sinned, that is, had done not what he, but what itself willed even by that same volition of the creature, by which what the Creator did not will was done, God accomplished his own design." Wisely employing like one supremely good, even evil, for the damnation of those whom he justly predestinated to punishment, and for their salvation whom he benignly predestinated to pardon. For, in so far as they were concerned, they did what God did not will; but in reference to the *omnipotence* of God, it was impossible they could do this; inasmuch, as by this very acting against God's will, his will concerning themselves, was performed. "Therefore, the great works of the Lord are immaculate in respect of all his volitions, so that in a wonderful and ineffable way, even that which is against his will does not happen without his will; because it would not happen if he did not allow it; nor does he allow it unwillingly, but willingly. Nor, as good, could he allow evil to be done, unless as omnipotent he could bring good out of it."

As to the Scripture examples which you adduce, they are just as much to the purpose, as mixing wine with oil. God, by Ezekiel, addressing the disobedient Jews, says, "Go ye, serve every man idols." I acknowledge, indeed, that this is not a word of command, but of rejection of the impious mixture by which the Jews adulterated his legitimate worship. But what more will you infer from this, except that God sometimes permits what he reprobates and condemns; as if, indeed, it were not universally agreed, that in such forms of expression, God sometimes commands, and sometimes permits. He says, in the law, *six shalt thou work*; it is a concession; for, consecrating to himself the seventh day, he left men free on the other six. In another way too he anciently allowed divorce to the Jews, which he by no means approved. Here he indignantly devotes the hypocritical and perfidious to idols; because he would not have his name profaned. But how does it come that you forget that the point in debate is the *secret providence of God*, by which he destines and turns all the agitations of the world, to his own purpose according to his pleasure?

Moreover, by corrupting another passage, so unskillfully and so perversely, you show that nothing is sacred to an impious and profane man. God's words are, "Because they were unwilling to obey my precepts, I gave them precepts not good." Here you trifle by telling us, that when they were deserted by God, they fell into idolatry. Whereas, there is no doubt God means the Jews were bound in servitude by the Chaldeans, who compelled them to obey their tyrannical laws. Now the question is, whether God merely permitted the Jews to be hauled by the Chaldeans into exile; or whether he employed them as his chosen instruments for chastising the sins of his people. Indeed, if you still seek a pretext, in the permission of God, all the prophets must be consigned to the flames, who declare at one time, that Satan is sent by God to deceive; at another that the Chaldeans, or Assyrians are sent to ravage. Again they tell us that the same God hissed for the Egyptians, when about to employ their agency; that the Assyrians were his mercenaries; that Nebuchadnezzar was his servant in spoiling Egypt; and that the Assyrians were the axe in his hand, and the rod of his anger, in the destruction of Judea. Lest I should be tedious, I omit innumerable other instances.

You are guilty of not less than *drunken audacity* when you pretend that God sends a spirit of error to the unbelieving that they should believe a lie, merely, inasmuch, as he *allows* false teachers to exist. When you prate in this way, do you suppose that your readers are so blind as not to see a totally different meaning in Paul's words, "God sent strong delusion?" But it is not wonderful that he should babble in this way licentiously, who either supposes there are no divine judgments at all, or securely despises the very meaning of the word *judgment*. For no one of sound intellect will say that a judge does nothing when he inflicts punishment, or that he inefficiently leaves to others, what is peculiar to his own office.

But it is in vain that you strive to alarm, and harass me, with your barking. You allege there are by the permission of God, erroneous spirits teaching that God wills sin. As the very same reproach was cast on Paul, by men of your stamp, there is no reason why I should take it amiss, to be associated with him. You quote from Zechariah, that God was incensed against those nations that vexed the Israelites more cruelly, than his displeasure would tolerate. Are you then so absurd, as to suppose there was not strength enough in God, to prohibit these injuries, if it was his pleasure that his people should be chastised more mildly? You will object that such is the sound of the words. But you are three, yes four times stupid if you do not perceive that in one way God wonderfully tries the patience of his own by a severe ordeal; and meanwhile, in another, is displeased with the insolence of the enemy, when he beholds him extravagantly exulting in victory, and rushing into barbarity. Besides, nothing is more evident than that your follies, if let alone, mutually destroy each other. For God either commanded, or permitted, those profane nations, gently to chastise the Jews. If you answer there was a command, I maintain, however causelessly troublesome, those neighbors may have been to God's unhappy exiles, yet they would have been free from blame, provided they had kept due bounds. For who would make a fault of their obedience to God? Yet you make a distinction between permission and command, inasmuch as when God had ordered them to inflict light punishment on his people, they by his permission exceeded their limits. On this principle, the Israelites were worthy of reproof, because they afflicted their brethren more grievously, than the divine anger allowed. Now your absurdity is too blind, in imagining they would have been free from blame, if they had only kept the due mean. For I will always drag you back to this point, that the Israelites were not merely guilty by divine permission (as you fancy,) of excessive harshness, but also of unjustly taking up arms against their brethren. You scruple not to assert that there was nothing wrong in undertaking the war, because God was angry at the Jews, and armed the Israelites to execute his commanded vengeance. But I maintain they sinned twice, because in the first place, they had no intention of obeying God. However, they were the instruments of his vengeance; and then, the very atrocity they displayed, showed that righteousness was not in all their thoughts.

Besides, in your principle itself, you display shameful ignorance in fancying that men slip and err, by God's permission, in so far as they are concerned. For it is an impious and sacrilegious figment that God permits any evil to men in respect of them, since it is evident he severely prohibits and forbids whatever is contrary to his commands. But why he chooses to allow men to err, no, *dooms* those to error in his secret decree, whom he commands to hold the straight course,—of this it is the part of sober modesty to be ignorant; while it belongs to mad temerity to cavil about it as you do.

As to Christ's permission to his disciples to depart, you may infer how skillfully you interpret the passage, from the fact, that he exhorts them to perseverance by setting before them the defection of others. For when he mournfully asks them, (John 6:67,) "will ye also go away?" he, as it were, puts a bridle on them to prevent them wandering with apostates. Does this way of speaking seem to you *a permission*? I acknowledge, indeed, that common sense dictates a difference between ordering and permitting, but on this point we have no discussion. The question is, whether God inactively beholds what is done on earth, or whether he governs with supreme sway all the actions of men.

Or, if the word permission pleases you so much, answer, is the permission *willing* or *unwilling*? This last supposition is overthrown by what we read in the Psalm, that *God does whatever he pleases*. But if it is a willing permission, then you cannot, without impiety, fancy him inactive. Therefore it follows, he regulates by his counsel, what he chooses shall come to pass.

Now it is too silly in you, to think of subjecting so sublime a mystery of God, to the rule of common sense. For, as to your objection, that Christ accommodated all his instructions on divine things, to common sense, he himself expressly denies it and convicts you both of lying, and impudence. Do you not hear how he declares, that he spoke in parables, that men in general by hearing, might not hear? It is true, indeed, that the Holy Spirit, always as it were stammers, like a nurse for our sakes; but common sense is still very far from being a fit judge of that doctrine, which transcends the capacity of angels. Paul exclaims, *that the natural man perceiveth not the things of God.* Therefore, he enjoins all who would advance in the celestial school, to become fools, and to be emptied of their own sense. Lastly, God everywhere claims for himself the light of intelligence; and time and paper would fail, were I to gather the proofs, which so convict common sense of blindness, that whoever would learn of God, must renounce his own wisdom, and seek light from heaven. Therefore, one example is sufficient. Paul calls it a mystery hid from ages, yes, concealed from the celestial angels themselves, that God would not have evangelical doctrine promulgated to the Gentiles until the coming of Christ. You thrust forward common sense, to subvert this doctrine at its pleasure, as you allow nothing to be susceptible of proof of which it is not the judge and the arbiter. The prophet, speaking of the *Providence of God*, exclaims, *how magnificent are thy works, O Jehovah, thy thoughts are very deep.* You deny anything to be divine, which you cannot measure with your own reason. What then is the meaning of Paul, when speaking on this subject, he says, "O man, who art thou?" Again, "O the height and the depth!" He enjoins wonder and astonishment, because all our penetration fails us when brought to the incomprehensible counsel of God. But you will admit nothing that is not subjected to your eyes.

THE FOURTH ARTICLE

That all the crimes, which any man commits, are the good and just works of God.

The Dissenter against the Fourth Article

Against the fourth, they loudly urge that passage in Isaiah, "Woe to them who call good evil, and evil good." If sin is a good and just work of God, it follows, that justice is an evil and unjust work of God; for justice is entirely contrary to sin. If sin is just, it follows that injustice is just; for sin is injustice. If sin is a work of God, it follows that God commits sin; and if he commits sin, he is the servant of sin, according to the doctrine of Christ. If sin is a work of God, and Christ came to abolish sin, he came to abolish a work of God. But if Christ came to abolish the works of the Devil, as Peter testifies, what are the works of the Devil? If sin is a just work of God, God hates and punishes his own just work; therefore he is unjust.

But if it is objected to them, that sin is not sin in God, it is demanded, in whom then is it sin? Or why does God himself hate it? Or why is sin called sin, unless it is because it is against the law, not of men, but of God? If sin is the work of God, God commits sin, and if God commits sin, he sins; as he who does righteousness, is righteous. But if God sins, why does he forbid others to sin? Why does he not rather command men to sin, that they may be his own imitators? For children should follow their parent. "Be ye holy," says he, "for I am holy." Therefore by the same rule it will be said," Commit ye sin, for I commit sin."

Calvin's Reply

In the fourth article you add to your forgeries; of which fact, I would have readers warned, only on this account, that they may judge of the matter by its own merits instead of by your odious calumnies. Not that I shrink from your objection, I merely complain that my language is changed for the malignant purpose of distorting my doctrine into something odious. You contend with me just as if I had said that sin is a just work of God; a sentiment uniformly held up to detestation, in all my writings. Therefore, just in proportion as your juvenile words seem subtle to yourself is in reality ridiculous. You infer that justice is evil, injustice good, that God is the servant of sin, and unjustly punishes what he does himself; all which are monsters fabricated in your own brain, and diligently refuted by me as my books testify. But you shall incidentally feel how detestable is the crime, to trifle in your railing way with the hidden mysteries of God. Now that you may know you have no business or controversy with me, but with that celestial Judge, whose tribunal you shall not escape; Job, by no other surely than the Spirit's impulse, declares that to have been the work of God which was done both by Satan and by robbers. Yet he does not tax God with sin but *blesses* his holy name. It is certain that the selling of innocent Joseph by his brethren was an atrocious crime; yet Joseph ascribing the same work to God, contemplates his immense goodness, in it giving food to his father's family. When Isaiah calls the Assyrians *the rod in the hand of God*, he makes God the author of the horrible carnage, which through him was to be effected, but without casting the smallest stain on God. Jeremiah, cursing those who did the work of God negligently, means *by the work of God* whatsoever cruelty an impious adversary inflicted on the Jews. Now expostulate with him, as if he said that God sinned.

Lastly, all who are acquainted with the Scriptures, are aware that such testimonies might be multiplied so as to form a volume. But what need is there of words when the thing is clear of itself. Was it not an illustrious display of the grace of God that he did not spare his Son? Of Christ too that he gave himself up? Here you, with impure and sacrilegious mouth, affirm that God sinned, if the sacrifice of his only begotten Son was his work. But every pious man along with Augustine has no difficulty in untying this knot. When the Father delivered up the Son, and the Lord his own body, and Judas his Lord, why in this surrender (*cf.* 48 Ep. to Vin.) is God just and man guilty? If not because in the one thing which they did, the causes were different on account of what they did. Therefore, Peter does not scruple openly to assert (Acts 4:28) that Pilate, Judas, and the rest of the wicked, did what the counsel and hand of God had decreed; as a little before he had declared (Acts 2:28), that *Christ was delivered by the determinate counsel and foreknowledge of God.* If you quibble about the word *foreknowledge*, you are abundantly refuted by the determinate counsel and the former passage leaves not the shadow of doubt, when it declares that Pilate and the wicked did, what the counsel and the hand of God, had decreed to be done. If you do not comprehend so great a secret, wonder with the apostle, and exclaim, *O the height!* but do not madly insult him. If you would be teachable, a fuller explanation is ready for you in my other writings; it is now sufficient to beat down your insolence, lest weak minds should be shaken.

THE FIFTH AND SIXTH ARTICLES

The Fifth Article

That no adultery, theft, or homicide, is committed, without the will of God being concerned. (Ins. Cap. 14. Distin. 44).

The Sixth Article

The Scripture openly testifies that crimes are appointed not merely by the will, but by the authority of God.

The Dissenter Against the Fifth and Sixth Articles

Against the fifth and the sixth, your adversaries say many things, and these especially. If God wills sin, and is the author of sin, God himself is to be punished. For sin should be visited altogether on its author. If God wills sin, the Devil does not will sin; for the Devil is in all things contrary to God. If God wills sin, he loves sin; and if he loves sin he hates righteousness. If

God wills sin, he is worse than many men, for many men are unwilling to sin. No, the nearer anyone approaches the nature of God the less he wills sin. Why then does Paul say, *the good I would I do not; but the evil I would not, that I do?* Why does not Paul will, what God wills (Or why does Paul will what God does not will)? Lastly, they demand what Scripture testifies that crimes are appointed not merely by the will but by the authority of God?

Calvin's Reply

It was owing to that very divine providence which you oppose, that you happened to mark the passage in the fifth article. Readers will perceive, that I am there reciting in the person of my adversaries the objections which are ordinarily brought against my doctrine. You snatch at that mutilated passage; and do you not deserve that everyone should spit in your face? In the sixth article, though you do not specify the place, your impudence makes a still wider bound, that I, who, as often as sin is mentioned, uniformly give the most solemn warnings. That the name of God must be kept wide apart, that I should anywhere have said, that crimes are perpetrated not only by the will, but by the authority of God. Certainly I shall willingly suffer anything to be said against a blasphemy so prodigious, only let not my name be so unrighteously coupled with it. How far you succeed in deceiving fools, I do not know; but I have no fear, should any one choose to compare your figments with my writings, but your dishonesty will render you execrable as you deserve to be. You contend if God loves sin, he hates righteousness, and you bring forward many things of the same import. For what purpose if not to subscribe my language? For it is not yesterday for the first time, nor the day before, but many years since, I have distinctly used this language, (*cf.* book on *Eternal Predestination*), "If in the spoiling of Job, there was a work common to God, to Satan, and to robbers, how shall God be exempted from whatever blame belongs to Satan and his instruments? Beyond all question, human actions are distinguished by their object and design, so that his cruelty is condemned, who digs out crows' eyes, or kills the stork, while the merit of the Judge is praised, who sanctifies his hands by the slaughter of the wicked. And why shall the condition of God be worse, so that his justice may not separate him from the crimes of men?" Let readers only run over what I there subjoin. No, let them peruse the whole passage in that treatise, where I dispute about the Providence of God, and they will easily perceive how all your myths are there sufficiently and more than sufficiently dispelled. Let them add, if they please, what I have written on the second chapter of Acts. When men commit theft or homicide, they therefore sin because they are thieves and homicidal. Now, in theft and homicide, there is a wicked design. God, who employs their wickedness, is to be placed in a higher position, for he has an entirely different object inasmuch as he intends to chastise one and exercise the patience of another; and in this way he never swerves from his nature, that is, from perfect rectitude. Wickedness being always estimated from the design contemplated, it is evident that God is not the author of sin.

The sum of the whole matter is this: since the cause of sin is an evil will in men, when God executes his righteous judgments by their hands, he is so far from being involved in blame, that he brings forth the light of his glory out of darkness. In that tract too, which roused these furies from deep hell against me, the following clear distinction frequently occurs that nothing is more iniquitous, or more preposterous, than to draw God into fellowship in guilt when he executes his judgments by the hands of the Devil, and the wicked since there is no affinity in their ways of acting.

Besides, I have published a work twelve years since, which more than sufficiently vindicates me from your putrid calumnies; and should have protected me from all annoyance, if in you and those like you, there were one drop of humanity. For, I do not boast how skillfully I have refuted that frenzy by which the libertines (those monsters) had fascinated many. It is certain I professedly undertook the management of that cause, and have luminously demonstrated that God is not the author of sin.

THE SEVENTH ARTICLE

What men do in sinning they do by the will of God, since very often the will of God is inconsistent with the precept.

The Dissenter Against the Seventh Article

On the seventh they ask, if the will of God is often inconsistent with the precept, how is it possible to know when he wills, and when he does not will what he enjoins? For if Calvin says we must always do what God commands, whether he will it or not, it follows that God would sometimes have his will resisted. For if he commands me not to commit adultery and yet wills that I shall commit adultery, and yet I ought not to do so, I ought, in that case, to act contrary to his will. Now, then, when he gives this universal command to the Israelites, "Do not commit adultery," where does he will that all should obey him, or that some should, und others not? Here your adversaries demand a more distinct reply, Calvin. If you say that he that chooses a part should commit the sin, and a part not, God will be inconsistent with himself in the same precept.

They also allege that God is a hypocrite, if he enjoins one thing, and wills another; that he has honey in his mouth, and gall in his heart. If it is objected to them that God has two wills contrary to each other, the one open, that is to say in his precepts; the other hid; they ask who opened that hidden will to Calvin? For if Calvin and his party know it, it is not hidden; if they are ignorant of it, why do they make assertions about a thing unknown?

They also maintain that two contraries cannot exist together at the same time in one subject. But to will at once the same thing, and not to will it, are contraries. Besides, if God have two wills inconsistent with each other, it is credible that Calvin (an imitator of God, of course) has two wills, and that he says one thing, and thinks another. Therefore we are unwilling to believe Calvin, as a man double-tongued, double hearted, and double willed.

Again, if God, when he commands justice, wills injustice, it follows, that the Devil ordering injustice may will justice. And if God, in saying one thing, and willing another, does not sin, it follows, if any one imitate him in this he does not sin; for to imitate God is certainly not wrong. Therefore it will be lawful to exhort men in this way;—lie, say one thing, and carry another in your breasts, that you may be like your Father, who says one thing, and wills another.

They also ask, with which will God speaks, when he commands us to pray, "Thy will be done;" and "whosoever doeth the will of my Father, who is in heaven...the same is my brother, and my sister, and my mother." So Paul says, "Thou art called a Jew, and resteth in the law, and makest thy boast of God, and knowest his will, and dost approve things that are excellent, and hast learned the law," *etc. etc.* Certainly, here the will of God is what the law commands, and if that will is good, whatever will is contrary must be evil. For whatever is contrary to good is evil. So in regard to the declaration of Christ, "how often would I have gathered thy children together, and ye would not." Christ certainly speaks of his open will, which had been expressed in so many ways. Now if he had another will contrary to that, his whole life was mere hypocrisy, which is horrible even to think of.

Lastly, they say, if God enjoins what he does not will, there are not too wills, but a lie; for whoever says he wills what he does not will, lies; and to command merely in words is to lie, and not to will.

Calvin's Reply

To answer the seventh is no concern of mine. Produce the passage, where I affirm that the will of God is very often contrary to the precept; for such a thing never came into my mind, even in a dream. But on the contrary, I have faithfully expounded, among other things, how the will of God is simple and one, though between his secret counsel and his doctrine, some seeming discrepancy *may* appear. Whoever shall modestly and soberly submit to the omnipotent God, will easily understand, so far as the scanty measure of man's intelligence may reach, how God, who forbids whoredom, and punished the adultery of David by the incest of Absalom, always wills one and the same thing, though in different ways. Therefore, lest the filth of your lies should cast the smallest stain on me, this may be briefly testified to the reader, that your allegations about me holding two contrary wills in God, are most wicked fictions of your own. I everywhere teach, that the most perfect harmony subsists between God's hidden counsel, and the outward word of his doctrine. I grant that Augustine mentions different wills; but these so harmonious with each other, that the last day will demonstrate how consistent he was in all his complicated modes of action.

This being settled, now fight with yourself to your heart's content, "about God forbidding what he wishes to be done, or enjoining what he does not wish, and thus commanding his will to be resisted." In all this filth I recognize nothing belonging to me. On the contrary, this is the sum of my doctrine. The will of God, which is expressed in the Law, clearly proves that rectitude is approved by him, and iniquity detested. And beyond all doubt, he would not denounce punishment against evildoers, if they pleased him. Still what he is not willing should be done, and forbids any one to do, he may, nevertheless, in his own ineffable counsel, determine shall be done for a different end. If you here retort on me, that God is inconsistent with himself, I shall ask in return, does it become you to prescribe the law to him of never transcending the range of your judgment? Moses proclaims that God has his own secrets, while the Law reveals what it is useful for *man* to know. Will you suppose that nothing is lawful for God that is not perfectly plain to you? In the book of Job after the depth of his counsel is celebrated, which swallows up all human comprehension, this clause is at length added, "Lo! these are the extremities of his ways, and how little is heard of him!" You will allow no counsel to God that is not brought under your eye. Now you are either more than blind, or you see that when God in his word forbids you adultery, he is unwilling you should be an adulterer; and that yet in the adulteries which he condemns, he exercises his just judgments which undoubtedly he could not do, unless both his knowledge and his will were concerned. If you would have the thing stated more briefly;—he does will that adultery should not be committed, in so far as it is pollution,—a violation of sacred order,—finally as a transgression of the law; in so far as he employs adulteries, and other enormities in the execution of his vengeance, he certainly does not unwillingly discharge the duty of a judge. For though we will not praise the Chaldeans and Assyrians for cruelly wading through scenes of horrid slaughter; yes, though God himself declares that he would be avenged on them; yet again he elsewhere informs us, that sacrifices were in this way prepared for him. Will you deny that God's will is concerned in that which he dignifies with the honorable name of sacrifice? (*cf.* Isa. 29 and 34; Jer. 46; Ezek. 39).

At length then awake, and acknowledge that when men are driven headlong by depraved appetite, God in secret and ineffable ways manages his own judgments. You think the quibble is subtle when you ask concerning prohibiting adultery, does God will that all should commit it, or only a part? For if I answer a part, you infer that God is inconsistent with himself. Now you have a definite answer, that God demands chastity of all, because he loves it in all. Yet experience itself, though I were silent, shows different ways of willing. For if his will were equally efficacious that all should be chaste, he would without doubt render all chaste. Now as chastity is his peculiar gift, it is easy to infer that he wills differently what he enjoins in the word, from what he realizes by the Spirit of regeneration. Nor on this principle, is there any reason that your shameless tongue should upbraid God with hypocrisy, as if he had honey in his mouth, and gall in his heart. For God pretends nothing either in commanding or forbidding; but sincerely reveals his nature. And in that secret counsel by which he guides all the actions of men, you will find nothing contrary to his justice.

Whoredom displeases God the author of chastity; yet the same God determined to punish David by the incestuous outrages of Absalom. Human blood he forbids to be shed, because as he follows his image with his love, so he guards it with his protection; and yet out of impious nations, he raised up executioners of the sons of Eli because he determined to slay them. Such is the express doctrine of the sacred history. If your blindness is a hindrance to you, yet all who have eyes perceive, that it is quite consistent for God to abhor whoredom and slaughter, in so far as they are sins, or (what comes to the same thing,) to abhor the transgression of his law in whoredom and slaughter, and yet to execute his own judgments, in taking just vengeance on the sins of men, by means of slaughter, and wickedness of every kind.

However dexterous you may fancy your query if there is any secret will of God, how did I happen to find it out; I shall have no difficulty in answering it, provided I may be allowed to follow the Holy Spirit as my master. For if Paul testifies that God dwells in light inaccessible, if the same apostle with good reason exclaims that his ways are incomprehensible, why may I not be allowed to admire his secret will though it is concealed from us? The wisdom of God is extolled in the book of Job, with numerous and splendid eulogiums, that mortals may learn not to measure that wisdom by their own apprehensions. Will you then ridicule all discourse about what is concealed? Or will you upbraid David with speaking foolishly of the judgments of God, when he acknowledges them to be a great deep? From all the prophets and apostles, I learn that the divine counsel is incomprehensible. I embrace what they declare with no hesitating faith. Why should this modesty be imputed to me as a fault? And think not to escape by saying, that I refer to examples that are not applicable; for surely I have the very same subject in hand as Paul had, when he exclaims concerning the depth of the riches of wisdom—the incomprehensible judgments, the unsearchable ways of God, in secret election or reprobation;—and yet ceases not openly to assert, that God follows whom he pleases with mercy, and dooms the rest to destruction.

Lastly, give up all fondness for your juvenile dilemma, for the Scriptures assure me of the secret will of God, asserting what I have learned from them I do speak of an ascertained truth; but because I do not reach so great a height, I reverently adore with fear and trembling what is too sublime for the angels themselves. Often, therefore, in my writings I admonish my readers, that on this subject nothing is better than a learned ignorance; for those rave like madmen who arrogate to know more about it than is fit.

You now perceive how confident I am about that will of God, of which the Scriptures are the witnesses; still it is secret, inasmuch as, why God wills this to come to pass, or that; and how he wills it, even the intellects of angels cannot comprehend; while your pride so far infatuates you and your fellows, as to tempt you to annihilate whatever eludes transcends your capacity.

Your objections about contrarieties are now sufficiently removed. You attack me indeed with this scurrility; if I am an imitator of God, you deny that any faith is due to a double-tongued, a double hearted, and a double willed man; but it is too foolish to annoy me. Incidentally, you shall know what it is to imitate the Devil, by ascending on high to become like the Highest. That which alone tortures me is the insane blasphemies wherewith you defile the sacred majesty of God, of which, however, he will himself be the avenger.

As the will of God, which he has delivered in his law, is good, I grant that whatever is contrary to it is evil. But when you babble about the contrariety of that hidden will, by which God distinguishes between the vessels of mercy and the vessels of wrath, and freely uses both according to his pleasure, you exhale a vanity as detestable as it is false, from the odious ditch of your ignorance. I confess Christ speaks of his open will, when he says, "Jerusalem, Jerusalem, how often would I have gathered thy children together, but ye would not," he casts the same reproach on the Jews, as Moses did in his song.

And indeed, we know that God actually performed what these words imply; since the doctrine of the law, the exercises of piety, and the various benefits by which God bound that people to himself, were nothing else than the spreading of his wings for their protection; had not their own unsubdued wildness hurried them elsewhere. When therefore Christ had tried so frequently, and in so many ways, to recall by his prophets, that perverse nation to obedience, he reasonably complains of their ingratitude. For in restricting your remark to the life of Christ, you display your ordinary want of skill, as if he were not the true God, who from the beginning had not ceased to spread over them the wings of his favor. Then, you infer that if he had another will, contrary to his expressed will, his whole life must have been a scene of hypocrisy; as if, indeed, it were inconsistent to allure by invitation and benefits, and to withhold from the heart, the secret impulse of his Spirit.

That the futility of this calumny may be more manifest, when he complains that he had been disappointed, inasmuch as the vine which he had expected to bring forth sweet fruit, had produced sour; what is your opinion about this, my worthy turner of sentences? Will you impute ignorance to him, to salve his reputation for veracity? The Jews disappointed God; therefore according to you, while sitting doubtful what would turn out, the event deceived him; as if truly a style of speaking, referring merely to the result itself, could be violently applied to the secret foreknowledge of God.

He says elsewhere, "you will surely fear me;" and they hastened to corrupt their ways. God promises himself some fruit from the punishments inflicted; he afterwards complains that he had been deceived. Can you disentangle yourself from this passage likewise, only by supposing that God is bound by, and dependent on, the free will of man? As if it were not sufficiently clear, that for the purpose of enhancing their crime, he assumes the character of man, who says that his labor is lost, when the result does not correspond. Undoubtedly, those whom God determines efficaciously to gather to himself, he draws by his Spirit, and as this is entirely dependent on himself, he promises that he will do it. Therefore as many are called, who do not follow, it is perfectly certain that that mode of gathering, which Christ laments as having been fruitless and vain, must differ from the efficacious, of which mention is made elsewhere, as in Isaiah (11:12, and 58:8; 43:5; 52:12; 54:7). "He will gather the dispersed of Judah;" and "the glory of the Lord will gather you." Also "I will gather you from the west." Again, "your God will gather you;" and that because he had just before said, that God had bared his arm, to make his power conspicuous in the sight of the nations. And therefore he repeats a little after, "for a moment I have left thee, but with everlasting mercies will I gather thee."

What I have said of the precepts, abundantly suffices to confound your blasphemies. For though God gives no pretended commands, but seriously declares what he wishes and approves, yet it is in one way, that he wills the obedience of his elect whom he efficaciously bends to compliance, and in another that of the reprobate whom he warns by the external word, but does not see good to draw to himself. Contumacy and depravity are equally natural to all, so that none is ready and willing to assume the yoke. To some, God promises the spirit of obedience; others are left to their own depravity. For however you may prate, the new heart is not promised indiscriminately to all; but peculiarly to the elect, that they may walk in God's precepts. Good critic, what do you think of this? When God invites the whole crowd to himself, and withholds knowingly, and willingly his Spirit from the greater part, while he draws the few by his secret influence to obey, must he on that account be condemned as guilty of falsehood?

THE EIGHTH AND NINTH ARTICLES

The Eighth Article

The hardening of Pharaoh, and consequently his obstinacy and rebellion, were the work of God even by the testimony of Moses, who ascribes the whole rebellion of Pharaoh to God.

The Ninth Article

The will of God is the highest cause of the hardening of man.

The Dissenter Against the Eighth and Ninth

On the eighth and ninth, they inquire what Moses means, when he writes that Pharaoh hardened his own heart? Shall we interpret it this way: Pharaoh hardened his own heart, that is, God hardened Pharaoh's heart. But this truly will be much more violent, than if you were to say God hardened Pharaoh's heart, that is, God allowed Pharaoh to remain in the natural hardness of his heart, because Pharaoh had refused to obey him.

In the next place, they ask concerning that passage, "Today if ye will hear his voice, harden not your hearts." Now if you interpret this, let not God harden your hearts, it will be very absurd, as it would be enjoining men to do God's work. For, if it belongs to God to harden hearts, it is impossible to command men either to harden them, or not to harden them; any more than to add, or take away, a cubit from their stature.

Calvin's Reply

Here again I entreat the honesty of my readers, to compare my language, and the whole strain of my teaching, with your garbled articles. In this way, when your calumny is detected, all the odium which you labor to excite will vanish of its own accord. Meanwhile, I do not deny, that I have taught along with Moses and Paul, that God hardened Pharaoh's heart. Here you expostulate with me to the contempt of Moses, and treating his word as of no account, ask, "When the same Moses declares, that Pharaoh hardened his own heart, why have recourse to that violent interpretation—God hardened Pharaoh's heart?" Now I need go no further for an explanation, than the ninth article, which while you quote, you either distort or misunderstand. For if the will of God is the highest or remote cause of hardening, than when man hardens his own heart he himself is the proximate cause. I everywhere distinguish between primary and remote causes, and those which are mediate and proximate; for while the sinner finds in himself the root of depraved feeling, there is no reason why we should transfer his fault to God. I have somewhere declared that to do so, is just to act like the maid servant of Medea in the ancient Poet, "I would," says she, "that the pines had never fallen in the grove of Pelion, felled with hatchets to the ground." For when an impure woman felt herself stimulated by her own lust, to betray her father's kingdom, this foolish attendant accuses neither her shameless passion, nor the allurements of Jason, but complains that a ship had been built in Greece. So when a man conscious of crime seeks pretexts of extenuation in remote causes, he ridiculously forgets himself. You now perceive though God in his own way hardens hearts, yet everyone is justly responsible for his own hardness, because everyone is hardened by his own wickedness.

The case is different when hearts are inclined to obey God. For as by nature we are all prone to contumacy, no one will desire to act aright, unless he is acted upon.) And yet when the Scripture says that hearts are prepared by God, and that the faithful prepare themselves to present to God, a voluntary worship; it is not inconsistent with itself, but shows distinctly that divine worshippers perform their duty spontaneously, and with the voluntary affection of their hearts, and yet this is not inconsistent, with God performing his part, by the secret influence of his Spirit. The case is different as I have already said in regard to hardening. For God does not govern the reprobate by the spirit of regeneration, but subjects and dooms them to the Devil, and by his secret government, so manages their depraved affections, that they do nothing which he has not decreed. These things, therefore, harmonize very well; that however God hardens whom he pleases, yet everyone is to himself the cause of his own hardening.

Lest I should be tedious, pious, and fair readers may take the help of this remark of Augustine, (Book fifth against Julian, chap. 3), "Whereas the apostle declares that men are given over to vile affections," this is rashly and unskillfully restricted to sufferance, because the same Paul elsewhere joins power with sufferance, saying, "if God willing to show his power, endured with much patience the vessels of wrath fitted for destruction," *etc.* And though that holy teacher had never spoken on this subject, the authority of God should of itself be more than enough for us. It is not I who have said that God takes away understanding from princes of the earth, to cause them to err; or that he held the heart of Pharaoh, that it should not be turned to humanity. I have not said that God turned the hearts of the nations, or strengthened them in hatred of his people, or hissed for the Egyptians and employed them as hammers. I have not said that Sennacherib was a rod in God's hand; but the Spirit so pronounces. What? When the Scripture also tells us that Saul was seized by a wicked spirit of God, will you refer this to allowance and permission merely? How much better is the judgment of Augustine, (*cf. Book on Holy Predestination.*) "If Satan and the wicked sin, it is of themselves; if in sinning they do this or that, it is by the power of God dividing the darkness as he pleases."

Whatever God openly declares, you impute to me. Let the same Augustine answer you for me, (*On Grace and Free Will*), "Scripture if diligently studied, shows not only that God is the Lord of the good volitions of men, which he himself forms out of evil, and directs them when produced to good results and eternal life; but that those volitions which retain their worldly character, are so in the power of God, that he by a most secret, but most just judgment, inclines them as he pleases, and when he pleases, either to confer blessings, or inflict punishments."

THE TENTH ARTICLE

Satan is a liar by the command of God.

The Dissenter Against the Tenth Article

Against the tenth, they argue in this way. If Satan is a liar by the command of God, a liar is righteous, and Satan is righteous. For if to command a lie is righteous, (as it certainly is, if Calvin speaks truth,) then to obey by lying is also righteous; for the righteousness of obedience is estimated by the righteousness of the precept. And as it is unrighteous to obey an unrighteous precept, so to obey a righteous precept is righteous. Now if Calvin is saying that Satan is not obedient in lying, that is, that he has no intention of obeying God. We will replay according to Calvin's own opinion, that this disobedient lying likewise, is done by the command of God; and that in this disobedient lying also, Satan is obedient; inasmuch as God has commanded him not to be obedient in lying.

Calvin's Reply

In the tenth article, behold against whom you hurl your virulent darts. For, it is no peculiarity of mine that you oppose but the dictate of the Spirit of God. So the Scripture speaks expressly, whom shall I send, and who will go for us; and immediately after, God, addressing Satan, bids him go, to be a lying spirit in the mouth of all the prophets, to deceive Ahab. Now bark as much as you please; you will no more bury the glory of God by your railing, than you will by spitting darkness the glory of the sun. Here too it is better to speak in the words of Augustine, than in my own. "When God testifies that he sends false prophets, and that his hand is upon them that they may deceive, he does not mean that his patience alone is concerned, but his power also." As to your prating about Satan not being obedient in lying by the command of God, it is not wonderful if you entangle yourself in many knots, by not acknowledging that God in an inexplicable way, so employs at his pleasure the working of Satan as to illustrate the justice and equity of his own government; without, however, freeing his instrument from blame, whom he compels against his own will to execute the divine judgment. Though your bitterness should rail a hundred times, this certainly is not the voice of Calvin, but of God, "I have commanded my sanctified ones." (Is. 13:3). Now if you imagine that God takes more to himself than is proper, he will himself find out a way to be freed from your accusation.

THE ELEVENTH ARTICLE

God gives will to those doing wrong; he even suggests wicked and dishonorable affections, not only permissively but efficaciously, and that for his own glory.

The Dissenter Against the Eleventh Article

Against the eleventh they allege: Calvin refers to God what belongs to the Devil, as the Scripture everywhere testifies. Now if God suggests wicked and dishonorable affections, and yet commands us to resist such affections, he commands us to resist himself. *Every good gift is from above, and cometh down from the Father of lights.* Are wicked affections even, a good gift? Does darkness (for depraved affections are certainly darkness) descend from the Father of lights? Why then is he not called the Father of darkness? James distinctly writes that *no man is tempted by God, but everyone by his own lust.* But to suggest base affections, is to tempt. Now as for your *salvo* about God doing this for his own glory, they say it is ridiculous, for glory does not ordinarily accrue from lying. When Nebuchadnezzar experienced the divine justice and power, in being changed for his pride into a brute nature, he ascribed glory to God, for he perceived and concluded that God is just.

It is God's pleasure to be praised by all nations; "praise the Lord all ye nations." It behooves him, therefore, to do those things, which all nations may be able to know and moreover praise. But no nation will ever acknowledge that it is just to punish men for what God himself has suggested. For we ask, if God should punish us for having a beard, would he not do us an injury; when he himself has given us the beard, and it was not optional whether we should have it or not? What man with a beard could ever praise him? Now if Calvin will say that this is the *secret Providence of God*, and to us unknown, we shall answer that God has indeed secrets unknown to us; but so far as justice is concerned, it is known to us and revealed in the Gospel. According to which revealed Gospel, (as Paul teaches), and not according to that hidden judgment of Calvin, God will judge the world. And so it will be understood by all, both righteous and wicked. For all, both righteous and wicked, will see that it is just that they who have disobeyed the truth, (not hidden like Calvin's, but open like that of the Gospel) should be punished; and that they who have obeyed it should receive reward. "The wrath of God," says Paul, "is revealed against all ungodliness and unrighteousness of men, who hold the truth in unrighteousness." But if the opinion of Calvin is true, the wrath of God is revealed against all the innocent. For if he suggests depraved affections, he is angry and hates them before the depraved affections. For to suggest depraved affections is a work of hatred; he consequently hates the innocent, inasmuch as sin springs from depraved affections, or rather, sin is depraved affection.

Calvin's Reply

You go on imagining monsters, that having vanquished them, you may celebrate a triumph over an unoffending servant of God. The passage where I have ever spoken in this way, you will not find; and therefore though I were silent, your mingled folly and impudence are alike powerless. If the wicked defile themselves by slaughter, adultery, rapine, fraud, I teach that this comes of their own wickedness; that God, however, who brings light out of darkness, so rules within them, by his own secret and incomprehensible government, as by means of their wickedness to execute his just determinations. If you oppose this, contend with God himself, who will easily receive your insane assaults. If you had one drop of modesty and docility, this distinction which constantly occurs in my writings, would undoubtedly appease you.

If the wicked examine themselves, the testimony of conscience will abundantly convince them that they must not seek elsewhere for criminality, because they find the root of wickedness within, in their own hearts; and yet God by swaying their volitions wherever he pleases makes a good use of their evil. Murmur as you please, I have now clearly shown, that in doing so, your quarrel is not with me but with God. I would hope that from the heart you did acknowledge God as the Father of lights, just as the Apostle Paul defines him, (1 Tim. 6), lest in your audacity you break through to the inaccessible light, No, lest in your sacrilegious insolence you turn that light into darkness.

Moreover, you absurdly infer from the doctrine of James, because every perfect gift descends from the Father of lights, therefore awful judgments that strike the pious with fear and trembling, do not descend from the same source. You still more absurdly ask me, whether I reckon vicious and perverse affections among good gifts; as if indeed the spirit of wisdom, judgment and prudence, differed not at all from the spirit of sleep and giddiness; as if too the Spirit of regeneration, which renews the faithful in the image of God, were none other than that evil spirit of God, who drives the reprobate to frenzy, as we read of Saul.

With similar shamelessness you clamor about my teaching that God executes his determinations for his own glory, by means of Satan and the reprobate. That Satan is the instrument of his anger, God clearly testifies both by his word, and by experience. Now with what design shall we say that God does work by the hand of Satan, if not to illustrate his own glory? You think you elude this by a witty retort, that righteousness is not ascribed to God on account of lying; but will you hinder God from bringing forth from your wickedness, the materials of his own glory? Certainly by nothing less than his outrageous pride could Pharaoh prevent the divine glory from shining forth, inasmuch as he had been ordained to this very end.

You allege that Nebuchadnezzar (Dan. 4:34), gave glory to God when he confessed his justice; and to show you with what confidence I despise your blunt darts, I willingly lend you a hand in this matter, and suggest what you did not think of. That when Joshua exhorted Achan to give glory to God, it is with no other design than that the latter should disclose the lie, and discover his own sacrilege.

But the question is, whether there is only one way of illustrating the divine glory, for if this does not shine forth by the lies of men, Paul must have been at fault, when he said, "let God be true and every man a liar," and immediately asks, "if our unrighteousness commend the righteousness of God, is God himself unrighteous?"

As to your objection, that God would be praised for his benefits, it is indeed true, provided you allow that the good out of which God brings and leads forth his praises is both thick and extensive. And here your pride, in ostentatiously despising the art of reasoning, is suitably punished, as you are always arguing negatively from the species to the genus. Nor will I honor with any long refutation your scurrilous jibe that God were unjust to punish men for having a beard, inasmuch as they only carry the beard which he himself has created. For who has ever said that iniquity was created by God? Though, he does ordain it in his incomprehensible counsel to just and righteous ends. Be gone, then, with that foolery of yours, of confounding the beard which naturally grows in sleep, with voluntary wickedness. Play the madman as you please, this will remain fixed with us, that they are justly punished whose wicked affections are ordained and directed by God to the execution of his judgments because their own consciences condemns them. And see how you entangle yourself; for while you acknowledge that God's secrets are unknown to us, you on the other hand, object that his justice is known to us. But if any one should ask you, is there any justice in God's secrets, or is there not, will you deny that there is any?

Moreover, how will you say that God's justice is known to us, when David and Paul look up to it with astonishment, because their sense fails them? Do the mighty abyss, and the rich depth of wisdom, in the judgments of God, contain justice in themselves? Why then will you deny that God is just, whenever the reason of his operations is concealed from you?

As a distinction worthy of notice, is made in the Book of Job, (chapter 28), between the unsearchable wisdom of God, from which the human race is warned of, and that wisdom which has been delivered to us in the law; so you also, unless you mean to confound everything, should have distinguished between that profound and admirable justice, which cannot be comprehended by the human mind, and the rule of justice which is prescribed in the law for the regulation of the life of man. I acknowledge that God will judge the world according to the revealed doctrine of the Gospel; but he will at the same time vindicate the equity of his secret providence against all wranglers.

Now, if you had the smallest experimental acquaintance with that Gospel which you prate about, you would easily understand how God remunerates the justice which is commanded in his law and never defrauds those of the promised crown who heartily obey his precepts. Yet, he justly punishes all the disobedient, whom he also terms his servants, because he has their hearts in his hand. In this way, Nebuchadnezzar, a furious robber and slave of Satan, is not without reason called by Jeremiah a servant of God, (Jer. 25:9). And if I have taught that God opens up a way for his own purposes, by inciting the hearts of men this way and that, why should the statement be imputed to me as a crime, when prophets have said precisely the same thing; these being in fact the words of the sacred history, (2 Sam. 24:1), "And again the anger of the Lord was kindled against Israel; and he moved David against them to say, Go, number the people."

THE TWELFTH ARTICLE

The wicked by their wickedness, do God's work rather than their own.

The Dissenter Against the Twelfth Article

Of the twelfth article they discourse like this, if it is so, God is angry with what is good; for if impiety is the work of God, impiety is good; for all the works of God are good. And if impiety is good, then piety is evil, inasmuch as it is the opposite of impiety. Therefore, when Scripture says, "hate evil," "love good," it enjoins the love of impiety, and the hatred of piety. They allege besides, that such an article savors insufficiently of a kind of Libertinism, and they are surprised you are so hostile to Libertines.

Calvin's Reply

I again testify before God, angels, and the whole world, that I never spoke like this, and that what was correctly spoken by me, is most wickedly and calumniously perverted by you. But if it seem absurd to you that the wicked should do God's work, upbraid Jeremiah, whose words these are, "Cursed is the man who doeth God's work negligently." Now, he refers to a massacre, which you will not clear of criminality, as it is manifest, it was prompted by avarice, cruelty, and pride. The Chaldeans were impelled by their own ambition, and lust of plunder, to forget equity, and inhumanly to wade through rapine and carnage. But as it pleased God by their hands to punish the Moabites, their wickedness did not prevent the execution of the divine judgment. Here, dog, your bark is, then impiety is good; as if God were impious, when he accommodates in his own wonderful way, human wickedness, to a different end from that intended by the perpetrator. No, you do not scruple to taunt me with the Libertines, a sect whose ravings have been by me especially exposed, so that I have no new defense to offer.

THE THIRTEENTH AND FOURTEENTH ARTICLES

The Thirteenth Article

We sin necessarily by the design of God, when we sin by our own, or by chance.

The Fourteenth Article

The wickedness which men perpetrate by their own volition, proceeds also from the volition of God.

The Dissenter Against the Thirteenth and Fourteenth Articles

Against the thirteenth and fourteenth, they argue in this way, If we sin necessarily, all admonitions are in vain, in vain are the people admonished by Jeremiah, "I set before you the way of life and death. Whoever shall remain ill this city, shall die by the sword, by famine, or pestilence; but he who flees to the Chaldeans shalt live." These things, I say, were declared to them in vain, if it were as impossible for them to flee to the Chaldeans, as to swallow a mountain. Now if Calvin shall say, that precepts are given for the purpose of rendering men inexcusable, we reply that this is futile. For if you command your son to eat a rock, and he does not do it, he is no more inexcusable after the injunction than before. In the same way, if God says to me *do not steal*, and I steal necessarily, and I can no more abstain from stealing, than I can eat a rock. I am no more inexcusable after the precept than before, nor more excusable, before the precept than after.

Lastly, if Calvin's opinion is true, a man is inexcusable even before the precept; so that there is no occasion for a precept to ensure that inexcusableness. For if the wicked man is reprobate, before he is wicked, that is, before he exists, *viz* from *Eternity*, and so sins necessarily, he is already inexcusable, and condemned before the precept, which is against all laws divine and human. For all laws condemn a man after the crime, and on account of the crime. Calvin's God condemned and reprobated the wicked before they existed, not to say before they were wicked, or had sinned; and because he condemned them before they sinned, he compels them to sin, that he may appear, indeed, to have condemned them justly. Lastly, Calvin, they here contrast your God, and theirs in this way.

The Dissenter's Plea of the Nature of a False God

A false God is slow to mercy, prone to anger, creating the greatest part of the world for destruction, and predestinating them not only to damnation, but to the causes of damnation. Therefore, he decreed from eternity, and still determines, and brings it about, that they should sin necessarily, so that neither thefts, nor adulteries, nor homicides are committed, except by his will and impulse. For he suggests to them wicked and base affections, not only permissively but efficaciously, and hardens them; so that while they live impiously, they do God's work rather than their own, and cannot do otherwise. He makes Satan a liar; so that it is no longer Satan, but Calvin's God, who is the father of lies, as he has often one thing in his mouth, and another in his heart.

The Dissenter's View of the Nature of the True God

But the God whom nature and reason, and Scripture proclaim is evidently opposed to the other, for he is prone to mercy, and slow to anger. He created the common father of all in his own image, like himself, that he might place him in paradise, and endow him with a blessed existence. This God wishes all to be saved, and none to perish; and therefore sent his Son to earth, whose righteousness more than abounded where sin abounded, and the light of whose righteousness illumines every man that comes into the world, while he exclaims, "Come unto me all ye that labor, and are heavy laden, and I will give you rest." He suggests good and honorable affections, and frees men from the necessity of sinning into which they had cast themselves by disobedience, and heals all manner of sickness and disease among the people, so that he never denied a favor to anyone that sought him.

Now, this God comes to destroy the works of that Calvinistic God, and to turn him out of doors. And these two Gods, as they are by nature contrary to one another, so they beget children equally unlike. The one produces children who are merciless, proud, savage, envious, sanguinary, false, thinking one thing, and speaking another, impatient, malicious, seditions, contentious, ambitious, avaricious, lovers of pleasure, more than lovers of God; in a word, filled with all bad and vile affections, which their Father himself inspires them with. But the other God produces men, who are merciful, modest, meek, benevolent, beneficent, abhorring blood, open, speaking truth from the fullness of the heart, patient, benign, placable, peaceable, abhorring quarrels and strife, despisers of honor, liberal, lovers of God, more than the lovers of pleasure; filled with all good and honorable affections, which their own Father inspires them with.

Such are the things. O Calvin, which your adversaries allege respecting your doctrine; and they advise men to judge of the doctrine by the fruit. Now they affirm that you and your disciples, bring forth many of the fruits of your God; for that you are generally litigious, eager for vengeance, tenacious and mindful of an injury, and tainted with the other vices which your Father inspires. But if anyone should say that this is not the fault of the doctrine which is sound, and does not produce such men; they reply that it does produce such men, which is evident from the fact, that many who have adopted that creed, are become such, while formerly they were not so wicked. Whereas, those who believe the doctrine of Christ become better; but they say that your doctrine evidently makes men worse.

Besides, when you maintain that you have sound doctrine, they reply that you are not to be believed. For, if your God very often says one thing, and thinks and wills another, there is reason to fear that in imitation of your God, you are doing the same thing, and deceiving men.

It is true, I have at one time, been rather fond of your doctrine, and have defended it though it has not been altogether satisfactory to me; because I have attributed so much to your authority, as to imagine it unlawful even to think anything in opposition to it. But now that I have listened to the arguments of your adversaries, I have nothing to reply. Your disciples, doubtless, attempt a reply, and among their own partisans, loudly boast of the truth; but when they close with your adversaries, they waver, and seek a poor protection in your books. For your reasons are obscure, and are almost entirely of the sort, which fall out of the memory, as soon as the book is laid aside, and yield no conviction to opposers. Whereas, the arguments of your adversaries are clear, keen, easily remembered, and apprehensible by the illiterate—the very description of men who chiefly followed Christ. Therefore it happens that your disciples, in general, lean more on your authority, than on reason. And when they cannot refute their opponents, they regard them as heretics, and obstinate persons, withdraw from their society and warn all to do the same. Now, as it is in my opinion, that we should attend to what is said, and not to the person speaking, so I judge that all must be heard, and everything proved, that what is good may be held fast.

Wherefore, O Calvin, if you have any true, plain, solid arguments, by which the adversaries may be repelled, I entreat you to publish them for the defense of the truth. You know what is written, "a mouth and a wisdom shall be given you, which none shall be able to resist." For my part, wherever I can lay hold of truth, I am prepared to follow; as well as to exhort others to do the same. But if by chance you are mistaken, I beseech you, Calvin, give glory to God. That will be more honorable to you, than to persevere in error. If you are just and true, I do not think I need entertain any fears about your indignation, on account of this epistle. In the first place, because it belongs to you to be informed of these things; and in the next place, because if you feel (as you say), that all things come to pass necessarily, you will believe also that it was impossible, that this letter should not have been written by me. Farewell.

Calvin's Reply

What you mean in the last article but one, I no more understand, than if you intended to confound human apprehension by magical mutterings. For what is it to sin by chance? And who, except yourself has conjured up such monsters? I have said somewhere, that those things which seem to happen by chance are governed by the secret Providence of God. Who will allow you to infer from this that sin is fortuitous? And then, as for what is found in my writings, did it originate with me? Or has it not rather God for its author? If the hatchet of a man cutting the branches of a tree fall and wound the head of a passenger, will you regard this as a matter of chance? But the Holy Spirit, by Moses, declares that such a man is slain by God.

Will you say that God, like one drunk, deals his blows at random, right and left, without discrimination?

Now, if you fancy that men sin without the knowledge of God, how will God judge the world? And if the transactions of the world escape his notice, how will he have the advantage of mortals? Because I maintain that God is perfectly aware of the sins of men, you go so far in your frenzy, as to accuse me of framing a false God. If I should grant you what you demand, that God is ignorant of sin, what kind of God do you pray he will be? And will you still boast that the people are with you, when depriving God of intelligence, and dignifying him with the same title that Lucretius did his images, you fabricate a dead idol in his place?

As to your argument that teaching is superfluous, precepts useless, admonitions vain, upbraiding and threats absurd, if men sin necessarily; if Augustine's book to Valentinus, "Concerning Corruption and Grace," a work expressly devoted to this subject, is not sufficient to dissipate these objections, you are unworthy to hear a word from me. As my refutation of Pighius, and your master Servetus, in regard to this calumny, is quite satisfactory to all reasonable and candid readers, I will now merely return this brief answer to your boasting. If you will allow God to command nothing, that man does not have power to obey, God will make it plain enough, when he shall place you at his tribunal, that he made no vain assertion by the mouth of his apostle, when he declared that to be impossible to the law, which he himself performed by his own grace, (Rom. 8:4). It is certain that a perfect righteousness is exhibited in the law, which would be prepared and set forth to all, if our strength were adequate to yield obedience to the commands of God. Now Paul declares it was impossible to attain to righteousness by the law. What dispute then have you on this point with Calvin? If you steal necessarily, you suppose that you are no less excusable after the precept than before. Paul, on the contrary, when he confesses that he was sold under sin, at the same time freely exclaims, that *the law worketh wrath*, because the shield of necessity is in vain held forth, when every man is convicted by his conscience of voluntary malignity. Tell me, when the hook was in your hand, of late years, for the purpose of stealing wood, to warm your house, was it not your own will that prompted you to steal? If this alone suffice for your just condemnation, that knowingly and willingly you snatched at a base and wicked gain, by your neighbor's loss, you may rave as you please about necessity, without being in the least justly acquitted. As to your objection, that no one is justly condemned, unless on account of crime, and after crime, I have no quarrel with you on the former point, since I everywhere teach that no one perishes, except by the just judgment of God. At the same time, I may not dissemble that a secret venom lurks in your language; for if the similitude you propose is admitted, God will be unjust for involving the whole family of Abraham, in the guilt of original sin.

You deny that it is lawful for God to condemn any man, except on account of actual sin. Innumerable infants are, to this day, hurried out of life. Discharge now your virulence against God, for precipitating into eternal death innocent babes torn from their mother's breasts. Whoever does not detest this blasphemy, when it is openly detected may curse me to his heart's content. For I have no right to demand exemption from the railings of those who do not spare the Almighty himself.

As to the latter point, do you not see how offensive your loquacity is? For even your master

Servetus, and Pighius, and such like dogs, would say at least, that those were condemned before the creation of the world, whom God foreknew to be worthy of death. You, indeed, will not allow him to doom anyone to eternal death, until such time as he becomes obnoxious to earthly judges, by the actual perpetration of crime. Therefore, let the reader learn how prodigious that frenzy must be which unhesitatingly subverts by jeer and banter, the whole course of divine justice.

It remains that I vindicate the glory of the true and eternal God, from your sacrilegious revilings. You loudly charge me with thrusting the Devil into the place of the true God. My defense is brief and easy. As all my writings clearly testify, that I had no other design, than that the whole world, should piously and holily devote itself to God; and that all should cultivate in good conscience true righteousness with each other; so my life is not inconsistent with my doctrine; nor will I be so unjust to the grace of God, as to compare myself with you, and those like you, whose innocence is nothing more than compliment and self-flattery. This only will I say, if any upright and fair judge should decide between us, he would readily recognize reverence for God, both in my writings, and in my life;

while everything proceeding from you, savors of nothing but mere burlesque upon religion.

Now, briefly to confound your calumnies, can anything surpass your want of principle in contending that God would be slow to mercy, and prone to anger, if he ordained the greater part of the world to eternal death? Beyond all question, fancy what kind of God you please, he alone is to be worshipped by all the pious; who, with the exception of the family of Abraham, suffered the whole human family to wander in fatal darkness, for more than twenty-five hundred years. If you charge him with cruelty, for determining that innumerable nations should be overwhelmed in death, while one family alone was distinguished by the life giving light; the answer is evident, that while the nations were spared from day to day, and the world was not swallowed up a hundred times in a year, just as often did God afford illustrious displays of his patience. Nor in truth has Paul any hesitation in praising God's lenity and longsuffering, even when he maintains, that the vessels of wrath were fitted for destruction, by his secret decree. If you are not satisfied with his testimony, I think I may safely despise your barking. For God needs no defense at my hand, but will sufficiently vindicate his own justice, although all impure tongues should emulously conspire to overshadow it. Wherefore, you and your gang, may hurl aloft your blasphemies as you please, to fall back again on your own heads. It is no hardship to me, patiently to endure your revilings, provided the God whom I serve is not reached; and I must be allowed to summon you to his tribunal, where he will in his own time appear, to avenge that doctrine, which in my person you furiously oppose.

Readers of any discernment will appreciate the value of your discourse, about the nature of the true God, when they observe that in all inquiry upon the subject, you make common sense the starting point. The existence of God, it is true, was admitted by all nations and ages; since the principle and seed of this knowledge, was naturally implanted in the mind of man. But how shall reason define what God is, when with all her perspicacity, she can do nothing but turn the truth of God into a lie, thereby adulterating all the knowledge and light of true faith and religion? The Holy Spirit commands us to become fools, if we would be disciples of the heavenly doctrine; inasmuch as the natural man is unable to receive or taste any of it. You on the other hand, would have the human faculty decide on the mysteries of God; and reason, which in its blindness, utterly extinguishes the divine glory, you not only set up as a guide and mistress, but presume to prefer to Scripture itself. So that, it is not wonderful if you allow the most opposite religions to be promiscuously confounded and esteeming the Turk steeped in the dreams of Mahomet, and adoring, I do not know what, unknown divinity, no less a worshipper of the true God, than the Christian, who with the unwavering faith of the Gospel, calls on the Father of our Redeemer. Now, although so many indirect jeers at all the first principles of our faith, do not aloud declare that you are the open, earnest patron of the infidels, yet your object was, by palliating the superstitions of all nations, to subvert the religion of the sacred oracles of the true God. From that reason doubtless, which is the mother of all errors, has sprung that God of yours, who indiscriminately resolves that all shall be saved. As if indeed, the word election which occurs so often in the Scriptures, had absolutely no meaning; when the law, the prophets, and the Gospel, everywhere proclaim, that they are called and enlightened to salvation, who were chosen in God's eternal counsel before the foundation of the world; and unambiguously declare that the fountain and cause of life, is the free love of God, which embraced not all, but whom he pleased. What do you gain by a hundred railings on the other side? You bewilder the simple by raising a cloud, about God wishing all to be saved. If this is inconsistent with that election, predestinating his own children to life, I demand why the way of salvation is not thrown open to all. That *eulogium* of the law is well known and celebrated, "behold I have this day set before you life and death." If God determined to gather all without distinction into salvation, why did he not *set life* equally before all, instead of distinguishing but one nation by this prerogative; and that for no other reason, if we believe Moses, except his free favor for those, whom he chose for his own.

You say that Christ was divinely sent, in order that his righteousness might super-abound wherever sin abounded. But this one word proves that you came forth from beneath, at the prompting of *Satan*. You insolently deride Christ, while you seek to cover up everything with the grossest falsehood, in the colors of piety. For if the righteousness of Christ has super-abounded, wherever sin abounded, the condition of

Pilate or Judas, will be no worse than that of Peter or Paul. And though I should say nothing of Pilate, Paul denies that the righteousness of Christ can be separated from the faith of the Gospel, (Eph. 6:9). Will you tell us what Gospel was in France, and other remote nations at the time when Christ lived on earth? What? Was God not the same before the coming of his Son? Why then did he seal up the treasure of salvation until the fullness of time? You must burst into laughter at Paul's doctrine, about the mystery being hid before in God, which was revealed in the promulgation of the Gospel. And now that the sound of the Gospel is proclaimed, the righteousness of Christ comes to none but those, who receive it by faith. Now, Therefore, have you faith? If you answer by hearing; it is indeed true; but the hearing is not independent of the special revelation of the Spirit, Isaiah (53:1,) exclaims in surprise, at the fewness of those to whom the arm of the Lord is revealed; and when Paul restricts the gift of faith to the elect, he refers to that passage as evidence. You allow no distinction. Christ indeed cries, "Come unto me all ye that labor," but he also exclaims in another place, "no man comes to me, except the Father draw him." Nor does he contradict himself, when inviting all without exception by the external voice, he yet declares that no man perceives anything, except as it is given him from heaven; and that none come to him except those who are given him by the Father.

Another passage you no less foully besmear, with your swinish snout; (John 1:4), alleging that every man that comes into the world is illuminated with the light of Christ's righteousness. As if John did not add immediately after, "the light shineth in darkness, and the darkness comprehended it," not intending to declare that whatever reason and intelligence had been given to men at first, were suffocated and almost destroyed; and that the only remedy remaining, is the light which Christ bestows on the blind. It is no doubt true, that Christ denied mercy to none that asked it; but you do not reflect that vows and prayers are dictated by the Holy Spirit; No that faith which is the fruit of gratuitous election, is the key which opens the gate to prayers.

While you are ignorant of these first principles, the denial of which reduces the gospel to a level with the rites of Proserpine and Bacchus, it is surprising that any called Christians should be found, entangling themselves with errors so enormous. As to your flippant insolence, about my disciples being like my God, cruel, envious, calumnious, proud, carrying one thing on their tongue, another in their heart, I will undertake to refute it not so much by word, as by fact.

As I have no delight in evil speaking, let your crimes remain unnoticed by me; except that I am at liberty, and it is worthwhile to testify before God to this one thing, that although I have fed you in my house, I never beheld a man prouder, more deceitful, or more destitute of humanity than yourself. That man is without all judgment, who does not perceive you to be, at once an impostor, an abandoned cynic in your impudence, and a buffoon avowedly scoffing at religion. I would gladly know in what you accuse me of barbarity; unless possibly you refer to your master Servetus; yet the judges themselves, two of whom were his zealous patrons, are witnesses to the fact of my having interceded in his behalf. But enough of myself, and more than enough.

What fruits my doctrine produces, not only in this city, but wide and far through many lands, I leave for the consideration of all. From this school, which you so atrociously assail, God daily chooses victims, of the best and sweetest odor, to illustrate the doctrine of his Gospel. The students there, (of whom the number at least is respectable), exemplify a painful abstinence, and yet are conspicuous for patience and gentleness; or discarding former luxuries, they are forward and contented in the practice of frugality. Denying themselves and the world, they all aspire to the hope of a blessed immortality. But because it is inexpedient for me to boast, let the Lord answer for me, by those displays of his favor, which he has given in behalf of that doctrine, which is in vain assailed by your odious abuse.

But I should like to be informed by you, respecting your character, when you favored this doctrine. You allege that it had not been sufficiently understood by you in consequence of your being hampered by my authority so that you held it unlawful to form any opposite opinion. You must assuredly have been too dull not to comprehend in several years what I both taught you familiarly at home, and so frequently expounded in your hearing in the public assembly.

Now there are many competent witnesses to prove, that although 1 failed in the various attempts I made to correct and cure your depravity of temper, yet so long as you kept up appearances with me, you were restrained as by a bridle; so that the cause of your alienation, may well seem to have been, that very licentiousness, which sought uncurbed, to break to the impiety in which you now glory.

You tell us you mind what is said, not who speaks. Would that you had brought yourself before this candidly to profit by the labors of others, and in this way to form a habit of docility. As it is, your only accomplishments being audacity and garrulity, you seek consequence for yourself, by despising others. For my part, I arrogate nothing to myself, but I think I have deserved this of the church, that if I may rank among the faithful servants of God, my authority should not be rendered odious. If you said that a few unlearned men hung on my nod, or were influenced by my reputation, you might give some color to your calumny; but now while you make it my fault that illiterate men are displeased with my doctrine, who will believe you that learned and ingenious men alone relish my books; No that such men are held thunderstruck by mere authority, from forming an independent opinion?

So far as your authority goes then, nothing is proved that is not rendered plausible to the vulgar. And this, indeed, is the reason why you deter all from liberal learning; and to gain more disciples, boast to your followers, that all study is vain and frivolous, which is employed in philosophy, logic, and other arts, and even in theology itself. You object that the followers of Christ were of this character; as if there were any inconsistency between literature, and the Christian faith. Here let readers observe the difference between you and me. I maintain that the wisest men are blinded by their own pride, and never even taste the heavenly doctrine, until such time as they become fools, and commanding their own notions to be gone, devote themselves in meek simplicity to the obedience of Christ. For human reason is utterly undiscerning, and human acuteness stupid, in the mysteries of God. Therefore, I say that humility is the beginning of true wisdom; a humility that empties us of all carnal wisdom so that faith may begin in reverence for divine mysteries. You invite illiterate men to come forward, and despising all learning, and inflated merely with the breath of arrogance, audaciously to decide on the mysteries of heaven; nor will you acknowledge any as legitimate arbiters except those who satisfied with common notions, stoutly reject whatever does not suit their fancy.

The Apostle Paul will easily answer another reproach, which you cast on my disciples, for they have his authority, for leaving you and such like *heretics* to yourselves; rather than by listening to you, voluntarily to pollute their ears with your blasphemies. You deny that such is the proper course, for that all should be heard. As if, indeed, there were no meaning in the command, to avoid a heretic who refuses to repent, after the second and third solemn admonition. If any man denied you a hearing, you would have some ground for complaint; but when you went away vanquished from the public assembly, at which you had full scope to babble, no, to which you had been summoned and almost dragged. What limit, I pray, will there be, if pious ears must be always open, until your appetite for God-reviling may be satiated? You take no ordinary pleasure in ridiculing all pious principles. Would you have the sons of God so stupid, as either to be pleased with your insolence, or to listen unmoved to your sacrilegious reviling.

So far as the cause itself is concerned I am confident I have so answered you, that all judicious readers may easily discern, that that Spirit has not been withheld from me, to whom it belongs to grant a mouth and wisdom, which if you persist in resisting, you will betray an obstinacy equaled only by your disgrace. I shall not cease to wish and to pray, though I dare scarcely hope, that you may at length yield to manifest truth.

As to your concluding cavil, that I have no reason to be provoked at your abuse, if I believe that your writing was necessary; it is indeed to my mind a serious and efficacious exhortation to self-possession, inasmuch as nothing is more useful, or better adapted, for bridling indignation, than David's admonition, "let him curse for God has so commanded." David, it is true, was well aware that Shimei was instigated by that same lust for railing, with which you now boil; but believing that the impetuous abuse, which the railer fancied himself uttering at random, was ordered by the secret Providence of God, the monarch is restrained by his religious convictions. For no man will ever endure with calm moderation, the assaults of the Devil and the wicked who does not turn his thoughts from them to God alone.

May God quell thee, Satan! Amen!
Geneva, 5th January, 1558.

www.ingramcontent.com/pod-product-compliance
Lightning Source LLC
Chambersburg PA
CBHW030929090426
42737CB00007B/373